Editorial

Complicity against Palestine

Wael Natheef was unable to attend the London Session of the Russell Tribunal on Palestine when it met in November. Although he had been invited to come and give testimony in person, he did not receive his visa in time to travel. As a trade unionist, he wanted to give evidence on the conditions of Palestinian workers and unemployed people in the Jordan Valley. He speaks with the authority of the Palestine General Federation of Trade Unions.

In the event, Mr Natheef sent a written submission together with a video recording. This was played in its entirety to the jury and public attending the Session. In a wide-ranging presentation (available online at *russelltribunalonpalestine.com*), he highlighted some of the working conditions endured by Palestinians. For example, minimum wage legislation does not apply to the 7,000 Palestinians working in agricultural settlements in the Jordan River Rift Valley. Of these, 35 per cent are women, while another five per cent are aged less than 17 years. Nor do these people have proper health and safety protection when climbing palm trees, working inside very hot green houses, or using pesticides. Mr Natheef also testified how, recently, the Israeli Exporting Company, Grisko, has started to label produce from occupied Palestinian territories as coming from 'Israel, West Bank Settlement'. Do not such prima-facie infringements contravene a number of European Union directives and association agreements between the EU and Israel? If so, what action is the European Union taking to uphold European law in these areas?

Of course, Israeli abuse of the rights of Palestinians goes much deeper than workplace practices in the agricultural settlements. Indeed, the first session of the Russell Tribunal on Palestine, held in Barcelona in March 2010, called on the European Union and its Member States to fulfil their obligations forthwith by rectifying breaches of international and internal European Union law with respect to the protection of human rights of Palestinians. The complicity of the European Union and its Member States in Israel's illegal actions with respect to the Palestinians were the remit of the Barcelona session.

The second session of the Tribunal, held at the Law Society in London, addressed international corporate complicity in Israel's violations of international human rights law, international humanitarian law, and war crimes. Over two days, it heard comprehensive testimony on a range of businesses trading in one way or another with Israel's illegal settlements in the Occupied Palestinian Territories. Who profits from this trade? A comprehensive answer to this question is provided by Dr Dalit Baum, project co-ordinator of 'Who Profits from the Occupation'. We reprint her written submission to the London Session. Close questioning of the witness by the jury elicited additional insights. Videos of these exchanges are available online. Dr Baum's work, using open sources, has proved so successful in exposing who profits from the occupation that the Israeli government has seen fit to try to introduce a law banning it.

The London Session heard extensive testimony of corporate complicity, which is summed up in an initial statement of the Jury, reproduced below. Full documentation of the Session, including the Findings, is available online. In addition, Alice Walker, the celebrated writer, shares her thoughts on the Tribunal, and why she sees it as a circle.

Certainly, the proceedings in London exerted a firm grip on the public who attended. The main hall of the Law Society was full for two whole days of detailed testimony. The Tribunal heads south for its next session in South Africa, which will consider the applicability of the crime of apartheid to Israel.

*　*　*

Blow the whistle

The contrast with the usually constipated Chilcot Inquiry couldn't be clearer. Hitherto, Sir John and his wise persons have failed to ask questions arising from key documents such as the Downing Street Memo of July 2002. As readers of *The Spokesman* will know, with respect to purported weapons of mass destruction in Iraq, the Memo noted that in Washington 'the intelligence and facts were being fixed around the policy' (see *Spokesman 105*). The Downing Street Memo and other highly pertinent papers were leaked in May 2005, during Tony Blair's final General Election campaign, and published in the *Sunday Times*. They have resonated ever since, but Chilcot's panel has, so far, been forbidden from mentioning them. Will they break this injunction, and bring us all a little relief, when Mr Blair returns for questioning?

Who leaked the Downing Street Memo and related documents charting Britain's road to joining the US war on Iraq? What kind of investigation into the leak was there? Was any one ever brought to book?

Now, five years on, we have the mother and father of all leaks. Private first class Bradley Manning, a 23-year-old US Army intelligence analyst, was arrested in June 2010 for allegedly leaking to the website Wikileaks a video of a US helicopter attack that killed at least eleven Iraqi civilians. Among the dead were two working Reuters reporters. Two children were also severely wounded. In addition to this 'Collateral Murder' video, Pfc. Manning is suspected of leaking the 'Afghan War Diaries' – tens of thousands of battlefield reports which explicitly describe civilian deaths and cover-ups, corrupt officials, collusion with warlords, and a failing US/NATO war effort. If he did, indeed, do so, Private Manning may have helped confirm the view of Obama's former commanding officer, General Stanley McChrystal, who, in the same month, was sacked for exposing US disarray in Afghanistan to *Rolling Stone* magazine – see *Spokesman 109*.

Bradley Manning has been held in coercive solitary confinement for months, ever since his arrest. He is not permitted even to exercise in his cell.

Also held in solitary confinement, whilst on remand in Wandsworth Prison, was Julian Assange, who, since 28 November 2010, has been methodically publishing on the Wikileaks website, and via chosen newspapers in several countries, the first selections of tens of thousands of US diplomatic cables. The cables, which date from 1966 to the end of February 2010, contain communications between 274 US embassies in countries throughout the world and the US State Department. Of the total archive,15,652 cables are classified as 'secret', whilst another 101,748 are 'confidential'. The remainder are unclassified.

It will take some time to absorb fully what these communications tell us, particularly about the nuances of US foreign policy. Certainly, some expose behaviour and dispositions that might not, otherwise, have been properly appreciated. In this issue of *The Spokesman* we reprint one cable in particular, which concerns the US military base on the island of Diego Garcia, part of the Chagos Archipelago in the Indian Ocean. This fortress, and what goes on there, are longstanding concerns of the Russell Foundation (see *Spokesman 81*). The cable in question, dated 15 May 2009 and marked 'NOFORN' (not for release to foreign nationals), reports US Embassy conversations with British civil servants in the Foreign and Commonwealth Office. The FCO absorbed the old Colonial Office during the 1960s, around the time Britain was sundering the Chagos Peninsula from the rest of Mauritius, as the emerging Republic sought its independence. Colonial attitudes persist at least in some corners of the Foreign and Commonwealth Office, on the evidence of this communication.

More generally, Noam Chomsky discusses with Amy Goodman of *Democracy Now!* broadcasting some of the cables from the US embassy in Israel, particularly with respect to Israel's onslaught on Gaza during the weeks before President Obama's inauguration in January 2009. Elsewhere, Paul Rogers considers what the US regards as strategic locations worldwide, ranging from laboratories producing antidotes to snake venom in Australia to cobalt mines in Congo.

This encyclopaedia of contemporary US government as it conducts itself around the world will, as they say, be poured over for years to come. Long may it continue to grow.

* * *

The Medvedevs

Zhores and Roy Medvedev are old friends of the Russell Foundation. During the 1970s, we published a succession of titles by the twins, translated from the original Russian. They included *National Frontiers and International Scientific Co-operation*, Volume I of the *Medvedev Papers* by Zhores, and *Let History Judge*, Roy's landmark history of the origins and consequences of Stalinism. In 1976, the brothers introduced our edition of Khrushchev's *The Secret Speech*, published to mark the twentieth anniversary of its world-wide publication.

During the 1980s, the Medvedev brothers were stalwart supporters of the campaign for European Nuclear Disarmament. Zhores, living in exile in London with his wife, Rita, travelled to the END Conventions in Brussels and, later, to Paris, where he addressed a packed seminar which hung on his every word about the nuclear catastrophe at Chernobyl. From Moscow, Roy sent a vital message of support to the Convention in Berlin whilst it was meeting during the spring of 1983. This provided some counterweight to the broadside which had already been fired at the Berlin Convention by Yuri Zhukov, then President of the Soviet Peace Committee.

Whenever we wanted to understand what was happening in the Soviet Union, or what is now happening in Russia, Belarus, Kazakhstan and the other successor states, we would consult the Medvedevs. So it is with great pleasure that we salute their 85th birthdays, which Roy and Zhores celebrated on 14 November 2010. We are pleased to publish for the first time in English the initial instalment of Zhores' experiences as a soldier and student during the War. The second part will follow in *Spokesman 112.*

University on the never-never

'There's nothing to pay up front' and 'you don't start to make repayments until you earn £21,000'. This was the desperate pitch made *ad infinitum* by Vince Cable and his Coalition colleagues as they scraped through the House of Commons vote to raise student tuition fees to somewhere between £6,000 and £9,000 per year from the current maximum of £3,290, beginning in 2012.

Many current students weren't persuaded, and demonstrated in outspoken fashion, bringing Central London to a halt week after week as the vote approached, as Jeremy Corbyn describes below. Their solidarity with generations of students to come augurs well. Many of those on the demonstrations will graduate before the full impact of the higher fees kick in. They know that they are already buried in debt; before any increases, the current annual maintenance loan is £4,950 (higher in London) plus tuition fee loan of £3,290, making a total of £8,240, or just shy of £25,000 for a three-year degree course. Many students take paid employment whilst studying in order to top up these loans, whilst parents and others frequently contribute if they can afford to do so. When two graduates move in together, their combined debts might easily hit £50,000. Currently, each one will repay their student loans at a rate of 9 per cent once annual earnings exceed £15,000. Interest on the outstanding balance ranges from 1.5% to 4.4%, depending on when the loan was taken. The lower rate tracks base rate so, when the Bank of England increases it from its historically low level of 0.5%, the interest charged on many current and new student loans will rise.

Current students understand full well that doubling or trebling fees will lead to individual debts of £40,000 to £50,000, whilst students of medicine and other lengthier courses face even more.

Then there is the sudden abolition of the Educational Maintenance Allowance. 'No new applications are being accepted for the scheme,' according to the official Directgov website. School and college students are no longer able to apply for such support whilst studying for university entry. Nobody now denies that the EMA has broadened access to university, but it has been swept away as higher education becomes a marketplace.

Lord Browne, Peter Mandelson's appointee and architect of the changes embraced by the Coalition Government, 'will allow the invisible hand of the market to sweep through the sector', according to the *Financial Times* (see box). Thus the state abdicates its responsibility for higher education, making way for 'private providers' of questionable competence. In the United States, which provides the model, there is already discussion of the failure of for-profit colleges and universities:

'As with the collapse of the sub-prime lending industry, the showdown between for-profit colleges and the government shows how the aspirations of the underserved, when combined with lax regulation, make the rich, richer and the poor, poorer. For-profit colleges provide high-cost degree programs that have little chance of leading to high-paying careers, and saddle the most vulnerable students with heavy debt ... '

Subprime Opportunity: The Unfulfilled Promise of For-Profit Colleges and Universities, by Mamie Lynch, Jennifer Engle, and José L. Cruz, Education Trust, 2010

Dynamite

' ... The proposals made by the former BP chief executive on Tuesday, are clear, concise, subtle and logically expressed. They are also dynamite ... Lord Browne wants to make students into consumers. He would expose the ivory towers to market forces by raising tuition fees, cutting subsidies, reducing central planning and making it easier for new institutions to enter the sector.

The review combines grand reforms that will allow the invisible hand of the market to sweep through the sector and smaller-scale interventions to ensure poor students and graduates are protected.

Certainly, no one will doubt that Lord Browne is serious about introducing market forces ... This scheme will create problems within the sector. Most insidiously, institutions that cater to poorer students will struggle to raise fees high enough to replace subsidy income. But cutting subsidies also makes it easier for entrants to join the sector – a stated aim of the Browne report. The proposal includes measures that would allow students who meet a basic aptitude threshold to use the loan scheme to buy education from any provider that meets set standards. The message is that students should be able to shop around. For this to happen, he proposes also to break up the central planning regime that decides how many places each university should provide each year. The current Gosplan-inspired regime would be replaced by a market ... '

Financial Times, 12 October 2010

Who profits?

The settlement industry and corporate involvement in the occupation

Dalit Baum

Dr Baum is Project Coordinator of 'Who Profits from the Occupation', and an activist in the Coalition of Women for Peace in Tel Aviv. She presented this paper to the London Session of the Russell Tribunal on Palestine in November 2010.

Who Profits from the Occupation focuses on exposing corporate interests in the Israeli occupation in order to provide accurate, reliable and well-documented information for corporate accountability campaigns. All of our information is public, derived from the companies' own publications, site visits and official documents. We have set up a database, www.whoprofits.org, listing hundreds of corporations and describing their specific involvement. Additionally, as an information centre, we provide on-going information support to dozens of campaigns, both internationally and locally.

Early on in our research, we set out to analyse the main areas of corporate involvement in the occupation. Our resulting three categories – 'Settlement Industry', 'Control of Population', and 'Exploitation' – have since become a useful tool to researchers and activists.

Israeli Industrial zones within the occupied territories host hundreds of companies, ranging from small businesses serving local Israeli settlers to large factories that export their products worldwide. The main factories are located in the three main industrial zones of Barkan, Atarot and Mishor Adumim. About two dozen settlements, especially in the Jordan Valley and the Golan Heights, produce agricultural goods, such as fruits and flowers, and sell them in Israel and abroad.

Settlement production benefits from low rent, special tax incentives, lax enforcement of environmental and labour protection laws and other governmental support. For example, all industrial zones in the settlements enjoy a special tax status usually offered as a special incentive to develop areas in remote areas of Israel. But the main settlement industrial zones are all very close to Israel's urban centers, and this gives them a competitive advantage over other industrial areas near the centre. Environmental regulations are hardly enforced in these industrial zones and tend to attract highly polluting factories that would otherwise find it difficult to operate inside Israel.

Palestinians employed in these industrial zones work under severe restrictions of movement and organization. All workers have to obtain special permits and gain clearance from the Israeli General Security Service ('*Shabak*') just to be able to enter these factories. And their dependency on these permits limits the workers' employment choices and makes organizing almost impossible. Israeli labour laws have been extended to Palestinian workers in the settlements, but not in full. With hardly any governmental enforcement or protection, especially given that Palestinian workers are effectively prevented from demanding their rights, employment under occupation is always exploitative, resulting in routine violations of labour rights.

Settlement production constitutes just a small fraction of what we consider to be corporate involvement in settlements. The intense focus on settlement production may obscure the fact that settlement industries are few, the revenues from them are very limited and, for all but a handful of agricultural settlements, they do not contribute substantially to the settlements' economic sustainability. Consequently, under the heading 'the settlement industry' we include the entire economic sustenance of the settlements. In addition to settlements' agricultural and industrial production, we investigate real estate and construction in the settlements, infrastructure and the provision of all vital services and utilities to the settlements. Israeli and international corporations build roads and housing units, provide services such as public transportation, waste management, water, security and telecommunication, provide loans, and market goods. The settlements' continued existence depends on services provided by these companies.

This wider settlement industry includes most large Israeli retailers and service providers. These companies claim to employ a policy of 'non-discrimination', meaning that they provide equal services inside the official borders of Israel and in the occupied territory – to the Jewish-Israeli settlers. Their intended services map does not include the Palestinian residents of the West Bank.

In other words, their policy is not only a policy of systematic discrimination; it is a facet of the ethnic segregation between Palestinians and Jews In the occupied West Bank. The settlement industry does not exhaust the different ways in which corporations benefit from Israeli control over occupied land; our mapping adds two more categories of corporate involvement. The second category studies corporations involved in Israeli control over the Palestinian population in the occupied territory. This includes the construction and operation of the Separation Wall and the checkpoints and, in general, the supply and operation of means of surveillance and control of Palestinian movement inside the occupied territory and between the occupied territory and the State of Israel. The growing global market of the homeland security industry has contributed significantly to the growth of the Israeli high-tech market. Often, the Israeli-controlled area is perceived as a testing ground or a laboratory for innovations to be 'tested on Palestinians'. We have seen this used by sales representatives of Israeli homeland security products as a blunt marketing strategy.

The third category of involvement points to corporations that directly benefit from the systemic advantages of Israeli control over Palestinian land, people and markets. This category includes the companies that plunder natural resources such as gravel or water in the occupied area, use it as a dumping ground for Israeli waste, profit from the exploitation of Palestinian labour, and benefit from access to the captive Palestinian consumer market.

For example, many Israeli food manufacturers and distributors benefit from selling low-grade products in the West Bank, while Palestinian competitors are stopped at Israeli military checkpoints. Similarly, telecommunication service providers exploit Israeli control of airwaves in the occupied land to illegally penetrate the Palestinian market.[1]

A word from the audience

'For many, the second session of the Russell Tribunal on Palestine represents an unprecedented and historic event in the history of international civil society's involvement in the Palestinian struggle against occupation, dispossession and repression.'

Teodora Todorova, ceasefiremagazine.co.uk

Reference

1 See our study of the Cellular Companies and the Occupation, in http://whoprofits.org/Newsletter.php?nlid=46

The Russell Tribunal on Palestine

London Session

The London Session of the Russell Tribunal on Palestine convened at the Law Society in London's Chancery Lane on 20-21 November 2010. Its jury issued this public statement following the conclusion of the session which examined corporate complicity in Israeli violations of international law. The Findings of the London Session are available online.

Over the past two days, the Tribunal heard compelling evidence of corporate complicity in Israeli violations of international law, relating to: the supply of arms; the construction and maintenance of the illegal separation Wall; and in establishing, maintaining and providing services, especially financial, to illegal settlements, all of which have occurred in the context of an illegal occupation of Palestinian territory.

It is clear from the evidence of witnesses that this conduct is not only morally reprehensible, but also exposes those corporations to legal liability for very serious violations of international human rights and humanitarian law. What distinguishes the present situation from others in which international action has been called for, is that in this case both Israel and the corporations that are complicit in Israel's unlawful actions are in clear violation of international human rights and humanitarian law.

The first session of the Tribunal, held in Barcelona in March 2010, found the EU and EU member states complicit in Israeli violations of international law, including: the illegal construction of the Wall in Palestinian territory; systematic building of illegal exclusively Jewish settlements on occupied Palestinian territory; the illegal blockade on Gaza; and numerous illegal military operations against Palestinian civilians, particularly during Operation Cast Lead in Gaza (December 2008-January 2009), which constitute war crimes and/or crimes against humanity.

Further, the Russell Tribunal on Palestine notes that the international community is clearly in agreement that Israel is in flagrant disregard of its international obligations; and further notes with deep regret that this wholly unsatisfactory and unacceptable state of affairs has been allowed to continue.

None the less, Israel's continued impunity and disregard of its state obligations as a member of the United Nations and bound by the UN Charter, has set it apart from the rest of the international community. Accordingly, the Russell Tribunal on Palestine draws to the attention of all corporations complicit in Israel's grave violations that their continued business activities place them on the wrong side of international opinion, morality and law. This clearly places both Israel and the corporations in a position in which they are undermining the very integrity and credibility of international law and the institutions that underpin it.

The main questions the jury considered in London were:
1. Which Israeli violations of international law are corporations complicit in?
2. What are the legal consequences of the activities of corporations that aid and abet Israeli violations?
3. What are the remedies available and what are the obligations of states in relation to corporate complicity?

Accordingly, in answering these questions, the Tribunal's full findings from the London Session will both summarise the key evidence that it heard about corporate complicity and identify specific legal and non-legal consequences and remedies.

The Tribunal has noted the failure of states to take appropriate action to put an end to Israel's violations and illegal conduct, despite the requirements of international law, or to hold to account corporate complicity in Israeli actions, which has prompted civil society to step in and take action to bring about policy changes that respect human rights and international humanitarian law. This includes a very wide range of actions in support of the Palestinian call for boycott, divestment and sanctions (BDS).

Corporations play a very decisive role in enabling Israel to commit war crimes and crimes against humanity. These corporate activities can, and have been, the subject of citizens' movements that the Russell Tribunal on Palestine received evidence about, including boycotts; shareholders holding corporations to account; divestments by pension funds of investments tainted by illegality; and actions that continue to put corporations in the spotlight with the purpose of bringing about change in corporate culture. In the Israeli context, civil society is taking effective action to enforce the law. Therefore, the Russell Tribunal on Palestine calls on states to protect the rights of all those who initiate or take such lawful BDS actions. Twelve corporations and the European Union were invited to participate in the London session, but all declined. Letters were received from three corporations and the European Union, which were entered into evidence. They will be annexed to the Tribunal's final conclusions of the London session. The Russell Tribunal on Palestine's conclusions include its findings as to the potential legal liability of several corporations, including the following:

a) G4S, a multinational British/Danish corporation, supplies scanning equipment and full body scanners to several military checkpoints in the West Bank, which have been built as part of the Separation Wall, whose route was declared illegal by the International Court of Justice in its Advisory Opinion of 9 July 2004. G4S also provided scanners for the Erez Checkpoint of Gaza. G4S operates in settlements, providing equipment for prisons for Palestinian political prisoners and for installations of the Israeli police in settlements.

b) Elbit Systems, a leading Israeli multinational, has an intimate and collaborative relationship with the Israeli military in developing weapons technology first used by the Israeli Army in its active combat operations, before marketing and selling the technology to countries worldwide. For example, Elbit supplied the Unmanned Aerial Vehicles (otherwise known as Drones) that were extensively and illegally used in the Gaza conflict. Despite this, the British Army has recently awarded Elbit a joint contract worth over US$1 billion for the development of the next generation of UAVs (known as the Watchkeeper programme). The British corporation UAV Engines Limited, a wholly owned Elbit subsidiary, will produce the plane's engines. A serious concern regarding the use of drones relates to their indiscriminate nature. This is illustrated by the fact that, for every alleged combatant targeted by drones, 10 civilian die. The Norwegian Pension Fund divested from Elbit Systems as a result of this complicity in human rights violations.

c) Caterpillar, based in the US, supply specifically modified military D9 bulldozers to Israel, which are used in: (i) the demolition of Palestinian homes; (ii) the construction of settlements and the Wall; and (iii) in urban warfare in the Gaza conflict; in all cases causing civilian deaths and injuries, and extensive property damage not justified by military necessity.

d) Cement Roadstone Holdings, an Irish multinational corporation, purchased 25% of the Israeli corporation Mashav Initiative and Development Ltd, which in turn wholly owns Nesher Israel Cement

Enterprises Ltd, which is Israel's sole cement producer, supplying 75-90% of all cement in Israel and occupied Palestine. This cement is used, amongst other things, for the construction of the illegal Separation Wall.

e) Dexia, a Franco-Belgian corporation, finances Israeli settlements in the West Bank via its subsidiary Dexia Israel Public Finance Ltd.

f) Veolia Transport, a French corporation, is involved in the construction of the East Jerusalem light railway. Veolia also operates bus services to illegal Israeli settlements as well as landfills where settlements dump their garbage on Palestinian lands.

g) Carmel Agrexco, an Israeli corporation, is an exporter of agricultural produce, including oranges, olives, and avocados from the illegal settlements in the West Bank. It also exports Palestinian products which are mislabelled as 'made in Israel'.

The Tribunal heard evidence that G4S, Elbit Systems and Caterpillar all acknowledge and actively boast in their promotional material about the use of their equipment during the Gaza conflict, which unlawfully inflicted loss of life and extensive and serious damage on Palestinian civilians and their property.

Civil claims against the above corporations, brought by victims of their complicity, are possible in the countries where those corporations are domiciled or have a significant presence; and corporations and corporate actors can be subject to criminal prosecution for breach of domestic law (for example, money laundering and/or concealment) and/or for the commission of international crimes, including the pillage of natural resources. In many countries domestic law incorporates international law, including international humanitarian and human rights law. This is without prejudice to universal jurisdiction or the jurisdiction of the International Criminal Court.

The full conclusions of the Tribunal's London Session will provide detailed examples of such potential litigation, and also highlight and encourage civil society/BDS actions that can achieve corporate accountability.

The Tribunal was impressed by the range and depth of the evidence given during the sessions. The Tribunal is extremely grateful for the time, generosity and courage of the witnesses, particularly those who took part at considerable personal risk.

The Russell Tribunal will hold two more sessions in the next two years. The third session in South Africa will consider the applicability of the crime of apartheid to Israel. After the fourth session, it will publish its full conclusions.

The jury of the RTP was composed of the following members:

Stéphane Hessel, Ambassador of France, Honorary President of the Russell Tribunal on Palestine, France

Mairead Corrigan Maguire, Nobel Peace Laureate 1976, Northern Ireland

John Dugard, Professor of International law, former UN Special Rapporteur on Human Rights in the Palestinian Territories, South Africa

Lord Anthony Gifford QC, UK barrister and Jamaican attorney-at-law

Ronald Kasrils, writer and activist, former Government Minister, South Africa

Michael Mansfield, barrister, President of the Haldane Society of Socialist Lawyers, United Kingdom

José Antonio Martin Pallin, emeritus judge, Chamber II, Supreme Court, Spain

Cynthia McKinney, former member of the US Congress and 2008 presidential candidate, Green Party, USA

A Circle

Alice Walker

A bout of flu prevented Alice Walker taking her place on the jury for the London Session of the Russell Tribunal on Palestine. As she recovered, the celebrated author of The Color Purple *and numerous other works set down her thoughts on the Tribunal.*

Nothing is stronger than a circle which is why, as Black Elk teaches us, everything tries to be round.

In many of my talks to young people, to women, to peace activists, etc., I advocate that in these times of planetary disasters and instability people everywhere should gather together in circles of friends, in each other's homes, on a regular basis, to talk through the fears and challenges with which we, as a world, are faced: more frightening events at this time than at any period in human history. It is time to circle, I advise, with the hope that eventually our diverse circles will engage each other, merge, and organically transform the earth.

I think of the Russell Tribunal as one of these circles, perhaps the most important, though its members may consider themselves strangers to each other. That they are not strangers is evident by their appearance, as a group, to take on the Tribunal's exacting and highly essential work: to cast the light of conscience on the behaviours of powerful interests and destructive players in the world community. This is a duty that calls out to those who understand how important it is to end our common silence about abuse and atrocities committed in our names, and who also realize that we must be determined in our efforts to care for the maligned and traumatized and oppressed of the earth. That this caring signifies our awareness of membership in the same clan, the same family. The family of humankind of which any oppressed person is the brother or sister, the mother or father, the child or grandparent that is, at one point or another of our lives also our own self.

It has been an honour to be invited to join the present session as part of a jury hearing testimony on international corporate complicity in the destruction of the Palestinian people, who, since I visited Gaza a year and a half ago, have become part of the earth's peoples to whom I have felt duty bound to show up for. What has happened to them has happened to countless others. Including my own tribes: African, Native American, poor European immigrant. It is because I recognize the brutality with which my own multi-branched ancestors have been treated that I can identify the despicable, lawless, cruel and sadistic behaviour that has characterized Israel's attempts to erase a people, the Palestinians, from their own land. For isn't this what the US military was ordered to do to the 'Indians' of America? Did not the British burn out communities of Scots and horrifically oppress the Irish? Did not wealthy and powerful Whites, generally, for a time, rape, kill, capture, and/or enslave Africans? And are not some of their descendants, at this very moment, stealing and confiscating African and Indian and poor white land, and harming people, using many of their ancestors' ancient tools of brute force and deceit?

It grieves me that I am unable to be in this circle of brave and compassionate people on this occasion because of a mundane yet tenacious visitor: the flu. Which condition, as I recover, I can almost consider absurd. Since college I have admired Bertrand Russell, the founder of the Tribunal, and also Jean-Paul Sartre and Simone De Beauvoir, early members. James Baldwin, as well, a person of such laser like intelligence and moral integrity, that it would have been a joy to sit in his symbolic chair. But the Tribunal will go on: because it is a living part of all of us. That part that knows what is right. That part that really does not appreciate wrong. That part that is not blind. Not deaf. The part that hears the cries of others in distress because those cries echo our own internal expressions of shame, horror, dejection and despair.

The Russell Tribunal is rare and precious and glorious, because it reminds us to act for ourselves, to follow our own conscience. To join with our fellow humans who are also awake. Or at least beginning to stretch and yawn. It is a treasure that makes the world not only more safe, but infinitely richer. I bow to its belief in justice, fairness, international standards of decency and law. The ability of humans to acknowledge and defend what is right and to do the work of holding the light in a world that seems at times to be sliding inexorably into the darkness. All that is ever needed to challenge that darkness is one light. May each of us, following the Tribunal's example, be that light, however small and flickering, wherever we find ourselves.

Diego Garcia

'Some rocks which will remain ours'

US Embassy
London

The daily release of
previously secret US
communications contained
this nugget, dating from
May 2009, about the UK's
official attitude to
preventing Chagossians
returning to their
homeland. We begin by
tracing the history of
Diego Garcia since the
1960s. In 2003, it was the
launch pad for the US
aerial bombardment
of Iraq.

During the 1960s, British forces forcibly evicted some 2,000 people from their homes on Diego Garcia and other islands in the Chagos peninsula. Formerly part of Mauritius, Britain declared the islands now to be the 'British Indian Ocean Territory' or BIOT. BIOT was to become home to one of the most potent concentrations of lethality on the planet.

Apparently concerned about the prospects of Soviet expansion in the Indian Ocean, the US government had asked Britain to find an uninhabited island where it could build a naval base. In return, the US said it was willing to waive up to $14 million in research and development fees for Britain's Polaris nuclear missile programme, the predecessor of Trident. At first, the Americans wanted the island of Aldabra, north of Madagascar. But Aldabra is a breeding ground for rare giant tortoises whose mating habits may have been disturbed by military activities. Fearing even then that ecologists would publicise its planned activities on the island, the US looked for an alternative. Eventually, they chose Diego Garcia, the largest island of the Chagos Archipelago.

Diego Garcia is strategically located in the heart of the Indian Ocean just south of the equator. But there was one problem. The islands had a population of roughly 1,800 people (who are known as Chagossians, but also referred to as Ilois). They had inhabited the 65-island archipelago for more than 200 years. Most of them are descendants of African slaves and Indian plantation workers. To deal with this 'population problem', British politicians, diplomats and civil servants began a campaign 'to maintain the pretense there [are] no permanent inhabitants' on the islands. The British officials feared that if the international community learnt about the existence of the population, it would demand that the Chagossians be recognized as a people 'whose democratic rights have to be safeguarded'. In 1965, British Colonial Secretary Anthony Greenwood warned that the evictions must be presented to the United Nations as 'a fait accompli'. In the same year, during negotiations with Mauritius over its independence from Britain, Prime Minister Harold Wilson insisted that Britain retain the Chagos Archipelago as part of the 'British Indian Ocean Territory'. Then, in January 1966, a British Foreign Office official wrote of 'convert[ing] all the existing residents [of the Chagos Islands] into short-term, temporary residents' in order to justify their removal to make room for US naval facilities planned for the island of Diego Garcia. Later that same year, in August, Sir Paul Gore-Booth, a senior official at the Foreign Office, wrote to diplomat Dennis Greenhill about the 'population problem' on the island of Diego Garcia: 'We must surely be very tough about this,' he said. 'The object of the exercise is to get some rocks which will remain ours … There will be no indigenous population except seagulls … The United States Government will require the removal of the entire population of the atoll by July.' In his reply, Greenhill says, 'Unfortunately along with the birds go some few Tarzans or Man Fridays whose origins are obscure and who are hopefully being wished on to Mauritius.'

Now, thanks to Wikileaks, we have another twist in this colonial tale. The US State Department cable, dated 15 May 2009, reveals some striking continuities with the colonial attitudes prevalent during the 1960s, not least with respect to keeping the United Nations at bay. That notwithstanding, the cable also tells us that the US government is profoundly sceptical about British proposals for a huge marine reserve around the Chagos Peninsula, which were to be announced by David Miliband in April 2010. Such a proposal might be used against our mega-military base on Diego Garcia, reasons the US diplomat who sent the cable almost a year before Mr Miliband's announcement . The Chagos islanders have fought a long battle to be allowed to return to their homes in the archipelago, if not on Diego Garcia itself. But it seems that British plans to thwart them, by establishing a far-reaching marine reserve, were not wanted, at least initially, by the sitting US tenants. The full communication is reprinted below. Meanwhile, the campaign goes on (see www.lalitmauritius.org).

With grateful acknowledgements to www.historycommons.org

*   *   *

Friday, 15 May 2009, 07:00
CONFIDENTIAL LONDON 001156
SUBJECT: HMG FLOATS PROPOSAL FOR MARINE RESERVE
COVERING THE CHAGOS ARCHIPELAGO (BRITISH INDIAN
OCEAN TERRITORY) REF: 08 LONDON 2667 (NOTAL)

1. Summary. HMG would like to establish a 'marine park' or 'reserve' providing comprehensive environmental protection to the reefs and waters of the British Indian Ocean Territory (BIOT), a senior Foreign and Commonwealth Office (FCO) official informed Polcouns on May 12. The official insisted that the establishment of a marine park – the world's largest – would in no way impinge on USG use of the BIOT, including Diego Garcia, for military purposes. He agreed that the UK and U.S. should carefully negotiate the details of the marine reserve to assure that U.S. interests were safeguarded and the strategic value of BIOT was upheld. He said that the BIOT's former inhabitants would find it difficult, if not impossible, to pursue their claim for resettlement on the islands if the entire Chagos Archipelago were a marine reserve. End Summary.

Protecting the BIOT's Waters
2. Senior HMG officials support the establishment of a 'marine park' or 'reserve' in the British Indian Ocean Territory (BIOT), which includes Diego Garcia, Colin Roberts, the Foreign and Commonwealth Office's (FCO) Director, Overseas Territories, told the Political Counselor May 12. Noting that the uninhabited islands of the Chagos Archipelago are already protected under British law from development or other environmental harm but that current British law does not provide protected status for either reefs or waters, Roberts affirmed that the bruited proposal would only concern the 'exclusive zone' around the islands. The resulting protected area would constitute 'the largest marine reserve in the world.'

3.) Roberts iterated strong UK 'political support' for a marine park; 'Ministers like the idea,' he said. He stressed that HMG's 'timeline' for establishing the park was before the next general elections, which under British law must occur no later than May 2010. He suggested that the exact terms of the proposals could be defined and presented at the U.S.-UK annual political-military consultations held in late summer/early fall 2009 (exact date TBD). If the USG would like to discuss the issue prior to those talks, HMG would be open for discussion through other channels – in any case, the FCO would keep Embassy London informed of development of the idea and next steps. The UK would like to 'move forward discussion with key international stakeholders' by the end of 2009. He said that HMG had noted the success of U.S. marine sanctuaries in Hawaii and the Marianas Trench. (Note: Roberts was referring to the Papahanaumokuakea Marine National Monument and Marianas Trench Marine National Monument. End Note.) He asserted that the Pew Charitable Trust, which has proposed a BIOT marine reserve, is funding a public relations campaign in support of the idea. He noted that the trust had backed the Hawaiian reserve and is well-regarded within British governmental circles and the larger British environmental community.

Three Sine Qua Nons: U.S. Assent ...
4. According to Roberts, three pre-conditions must be met before HMG could establish a park. First, 'we need to make sure the U.S. government is comfortable with the idea. We would need to present this proposal very clearly to the American administration ... All we do should enhance base security or leave it unchanged.' Polcouns expressed appreciation for this a priori commitment, but stressed that the 1966 U.S.-UK Exchange of Notes concerning the BIOT would, in any event, require U.S. assent to any significant change of the BIOT's status that could impact the BIOT's strategic use. Roberts stressed that the proposal 'would have no impact on how Diego Garcia is administered as a base.' In response to a request for clarification on this point from Polcouns, Roberts asserted that the proposal would have absolutely no impact on the right of U.S. or British military vessels to use the BIOT for passage, anchorage, prepositioning, or other uses. Polcouns rejoined that **designating the BIOT as a marine park could, years down the road, create public questioning about the suitability of the BIOT for military purposes.** Roberts responded that the terms of reference for the establishment of a marine park would clearly state that the BIOT, including Diego Garcia, was reserved for military uses.

5. Ashley Smith, the Ministry of Defense's (MOD) International Policy and Planning Assistant Head, Asia Pacific, who also participated in the meeting, affirmed that the MOD 'shares the same concerns as the U.S. regarding security' and would ensure that security concerns were fully and properly addressed in any proposal for a marine park. Roberts agreed, stating that 'the primary purpose of the BIOT is security' but that HMG could also address environmental concerns in its administration of the BIOT. Smith added that the establishment of a marine reserve had the

potential to be a 'win-win situation in terms of establishing situational awareness' of the BIOT. He stressed that HMG sought 'no constraints on military operations' as a result of the establishment of a marine park.

... Mauritian Assent ...

6. Roberts outlined two other prerequisites for establishment of a marine park. HMG would seek assent from the Government of Mauritius, which disputes sovereignty over the Chagos Archipelago, in order to avoid the GOM 'raising complaints with the UN.' He asserted that the GOM had expressed little interest in protecting the archipelago's sensitive environment and was primarily interested in the archipelago's economic potential as a fishery. Roberts noted that in January 2009 HMG held the first-ever 'formal talks' with Mauritius regarding the BIOT. The talks included the Mauritian Prime Minister. Roberts said that he 'cast a fly in the talks over how we could improve stewardship of the territory,' but the Mauritian participants 'were not focused on environmental issues and expressed interest only in fishery control.' He said that one Mauritian participant in the talks complained that the Indian Ocean is 'the only ocean in the world where the fish die of old age.' In HMG's view, the marine park concept aims to 'go beyond economic value and consider bio-diversity and intangible values.'

... Chagossian Assent

7. Roberts acknowledged that 'we need to find a way to get through the various Chagossian lobbies.' He admitted that HMG is 'under pressure' from the Chagossians and their advocates to permit resettlement of the 'outer islands' of the BIOT. He noted, without providing details, that 'there are proposals (for a marine park) that could provide the Chagossians warden jobs' within the BIOT. However, Roberts stated that, according to the HMG's current thinking on a reserve, there would be 'no human footprints' or 'Man Fridays' on the BIOT's uninhabited islands. *He asserted that establishing a marine park would, in effect, put paid to resettlement claims of the archipelago's former residents.* Responding to Polcouns' observation that the advocates of Chagossian resettlement continue to vigorously press their case, Roberts opined that the UK's 'environmental lobby is far more powerful than the Chagossians' advocates.' (Note: One group of Chagossian litigants is appealing to the European Court of Human Rights (ECHR) the decision of Britain's highest court to deny 'resettlement rights' to the islands' former inhabitants. See below at paragraph 13 and reftel. End Note.)

Je Ne Regrette Rien

8. Roberts observed that BIOT has 'served its role very well,' advancing shared U.S.-UK strategic security objectives for the past several decades. The BIOT 'has had a great role in assuring the security of the UK and U.S. – much more than anyone foresaw' in the 1960s, Roberts emphasized. *'We do not regret the removal of the population,' since removal was necessary for the BIOT to fulfill its strategic purpose, he said. Removal of the population is the reason that the BIOT's uninhabited islands and the surrounding waters are in 'pristine' condition. Roberts added that Diego Garcia's excellent condition reflects the responsible stewardship of the U.S. and UK forces using it.*

Administering a Reserve

9. Roberts acknowledged that numerous technical questions needed to be resolved regarding the establishment and administration of a marine park, although he described the governmental 'act' of declaring a marine park as a relatively straightforward and rapid process. He noted that the establishment of a marine reserve would require permitting scientists to visit BIOT, but that creating a park would help restrict access for non-scientific purposes. For example, he continued, the rules governing the park could strictly limit access to BIOT by yachts, which Roberts referred to as 'sea gypsies.'

BIOT: More Than Just Diego Garcia

10. Following the meeting with Roberts, Joanne Yeadon, Head of the FCO's Overseas Territories Directorate's BIOT and Pitcairn Section, who also attended the meeting with Polcouns, told Poloff that the marine park proposal would 'not impact the base on Diego Garcia in any way' and would have no impact on the parameters of the U.S.-UK 1966 exchange of notes since the marine park would 'have no impact on defense purposes.' Yeadon averred that the provision of the UN Convention on the Law of the Sea guaranteed free passage of vessels, including military vessels, and that the presence of a marine park would not diminish that right.

11. Yeadon stressed that the exchange of notes governed more than just the atoll of Diego Garcia but expressly provided that all of the BIOT was 'set aside for defense purposes.' (Note: This is correct. End Note.) She urged Embassy officers in discussions with advocates for the Chagossians, including with members of the 'All Party Parliamentary Group on Chagos Islands (APPG),' to affirm that the USG requires the entire BIOT for

defense purposes. Making this point would be the best rejoinder to the Chagossians' assertion that partial settlement of the outer islands of the Chagos Archipelago would have no impact on the use of Diego Garcia. She described that assertion as essentially irrelevant if the entire BIOT needed to be uninhabited for defense purposes.

12. Yeadon dismissed the APPG as a 'persistent' but relatively non-influential group within parliament or with the wider public. She said the FCO had received only a handful of public inquiries regarding the status of the BIOT. Yeadon described one of the Chagossians' most outspoken advocates, former HMG High Commissioner to Mauritius David Snoxell, as 'entirely lacking in influence' within the FCO. She also asserted that the Conservatives, if in power after the next general election, would not support a Chagossian right of return. She averred that many members of the Liberal Democrats (Britain's third largest party after Labour and the Conservatives) supported a 'right of return.'

13. Yeadon told Poloff May 12, and in several prior meetings, that the FCO will vigorously contest the Chagossians' 'right of return' lawsuit before the European Court of Human Rights (ECHR). HMG will argue that the ECHR lacks jurisdiction over the BIOT in the present case. Roberts stressed May 12 (as has Yeadon on previous occasions) that the outer islands are 'essentially uninhabitable' and could only be rendered livable by modern, Western standards with a massive infusion of cash.

Comment
14. Regardless of the outcome of the ECHR case, however, the Chagossians and their advocates, including the 'All Party Parliamentary Group on Chagos Islands (APPG),' will continue to press their case in the court of public opinion. Their strategy is to publicize what they characterize as the plight of the so-called Chagossian diaspora, thereby galvanizing public opinion and, in their best case scenario, causing the government to change course and allow a 'right of return.' They would point to the government's recent retreat on the issue of Gurkha veterans' right to settle in the UK as a model. Despite FCO assurances that the marine park concept – still in an early, conceptual phase – would not impinge on BIOT's value as a strategic resource, **we are concerned that, long-term, both the British public and policy makers would come to see the existence of a marine reserve as inherently inconsistent with the military use of Diego Garcia – and the entire BIOT.** In any event, the U.S. and UK would need to carefully negotiate the parameters of such a marine park – a point on which Roberts

unequivocally agreed. In Embassy London's view, these negotiations should occur among U.S. and UK experts separate from the 2009 annual Political-Military consultations, given the specific and technical legal and environmental issues that would be subject to discussion.

15. Comment Continued. We do not doubt the current government's resolve to prevent the resettlement of the islands' former inhabitants, although as FCO Parliamentary Under-Secretary Gillian Merron noted in an April parliamentary debate, 'FCO will continue to organize and fund visits to the territory by the Chagossians.' We are not as sanguine as the FCO's Yeadon, however, that the Conservatives would oppose a right of return. Indeed, MP Keith Simpson, the Conservatives' Shadow Minister, Foreign Affairs, stated in the same April parliamentary debate in which Merron spoke that HMG 'should take into account what I suspect is the all-party view that the rights of the Chagossian people should be recognized, and that there should at the very least be a timetable for the return of those people at least to the outer islands, if not the inner islands.' Establishing a marine reserve might, indeed, as the FCO's Roberts stated, be the most effective long-term way to prevent any of the Chagos Islands' former inhabitants or their descendants from resettling in the BIOT. End Comment.

* * *

The Mauritian campaigning group LALIT wrote to Princess Anne about Diego Garcia during her recent visit. We reprint excerpts.

'We write to you, as representative of the British Monarchy, on the occasion of your visit to Mauritius. The Monarchy that you represent has been the source of certain autocratic powers on which the British State has relied in order to perpetrate a series of actions which have caused great suffering to the Mauritian people, including the people of Chagos. Some of these actions have been illegal, others immoral, and all of them based on anachronistic decrees decided behind the back of elected Parliamentarians of your own country. We refer to the "Queen's Order in Council" made at Buckingham Palace, an "Order" that illegally dismembered Mauritius … There was then a so-called Immigration Ordinance of 1971, enacted by the Commissioner for BIOT who is appointed by the Monarch. This Ordinance banished the Chagossians from their homes. Since the 2000 judgment in favour of the Chagossians, and even as recently as 2004, there have been further "Orders in Council" that over-rode the decision of the highest courts of your land … The fact that your visit is one month after the coming into force of the Marine Protected Area and coincides with the publication of the Wikileaks documents makes the official nature of your visit all the more unacceptable … '

LALIT, 3 December 2010 (www.lalitmaritius.org)

Exposing Western leadership

Noam Chomsky interviewed by Amy Goodman

On 30 November 2010, Democracy Now! in New York broadcast a live interview with Noam Chomsky about what the leaked State Department cables reveal, from which these excerpts are taken. Presenter Amy Goodman started by reminding her audience of the leak of the Pentagon Papers on Vietnam, in 1971.

Amy Goodman: *... Forty years ago, Noam Chomsky and Howard Zinn helped government whistleblower Daniel Ellsberg edit and release the Pentagon Papers, that top-secret internal US history of the Vietnam War ... Before we talk about WikiLeaks, what was your involvement in the Pentagon Papers? I don't think most people know about this.*

Noam Chomsky: Dan and I were friends. Tony Russo also prepared them and helped leak them. I got advance copies from Dan and Tony and there were several people who were releasing them to the press. I was one of them. Then I – along with Howard Zinn, as you mentioned – edited a volume of essays and indexed the papers.

So explain how it worked. I always think this is important – to tell this story – especially for young people. Dan Ellsberg – Pentagon official, top-secret clearance – gets this US involvement in Vietnam history out of his safe, he Xerox's it, and then how did you get your hands on it? He just directly gave it to you?

From Dan Ellsberg and Tony Russo, who had done the Xeroxing and the preparation of the material.

How much did you edit?

Well, we did not modify anything. The papers were not edited. They were in their original form. What Howard Zinn and I did was – they came out in four volumes – we prepared a fifth volume, which was critical essays by many scholars on the papers, what they mean, the significance and so on. And an index, which is almost indispensable for using them seriously. That's the fifth volume in the Beacon Press series.

So you were then one of the first people to see the Pentagon Papers?

Outside of Dan Ellsberg and Tony Russo, yes. I mean, there were some journalists who may have seen them, I am not sure.

What are your thoughts today? For example, we just played this clip of New York republican congress member Peter King who says WikiLeaks should be declared a foreign terrorist organization.

I think that is outlandish. We should understand – and the Pentagon Papers is another case in point – that one of the major reasons for government secrecy is to protect the government from its own population. In the Pentagon Papers, for example, there was one volume – the negotiations volume – which might have had a bearing on ongoing activities, and Daniel Ellsberg withheld that. That came out a little bit later. If you look at the papers themselves, there are things Americans *should* have known that others did not want them to know. And as far as I can tell, from what I've seen here, pretty much the same is true. In fact, the current leaks are – what I've seen, at least – primarily interesting because of what they tell us about how the diplomatic service works.

The documents' revelations about Iran come just as the Iranian government has agreed to a new round of nuclear talks. Israeli Prime Minister Benjamin Netanyahu said the cables vindicate the Israeli position that Iran poses a nuclear threat. Netanyahu said,

> Our region has been hostage to a narrative that is the result of sixty years of propaganda, which paints Israel as the greatest threat. In reality, leaders understand that that view is bankrupt. For the first time in history, there is agreement that Iran is the threat. If leaders start saying openly what they have long been saying behind closed doors, we can make a real breakthrough on the road to peace.

Secretary of State Hillary Clinton also discussed Iran at her news conference in Washington. This is what she said:

> I think that it should not be a surprise to anyone that Iran is a source of great concern, not only in the United States. What comes through in every meeting

that I have – anywhere in the world – is a concern about Iranian actions and intentions. So, if anything, any of the comments that are being reported on allegedly from the cables confirm the fact that Iran poses a very serious threat in the eyes of many of her neighbours and a serious concern far beyond her region. That is why the international community came together to pass the strongest possible sanctions against Iran. It did not happen because the United States said, 'Please, do this for us!' It happened because countries – once they evaluated the evidence concerning Iran's actions and intentions – reached the same conclusion that the United States reached: that we must do whatever we can to muster the international community to take action to prevent Iran from becoming a nuclear weapons state. So if anyone reading the stories about these, uh, alleged cables thinks carefully what they will conclude is that the concern about Iran is well founded, widely shared, and will continue to be at the source of the policy that we pursue with like-minded nations to try to prevent Iran from acquiring nuclear weapons.

That was Secretary Hillary Clinton yesterday at a news conference. I wanted to get your comment on Clinton, Netanyahu's comment, and the fact that Abdullah of Saudi Arabia called for the US to attack Iran. Noam Chomsky?

That essentially reinforces what I said before, that the main significance of the cables that are being released so far is what they tell us about Western leadership. So Hillary Clinton and Benjamin Netanyahu surely know of the careful polls of Arab public opinion. The Brookings Institute just a few months ago released extensive polls of what Arabs think about Iran. The results are rather striking. They show the Arab opinion holds that the major threat in the region is Israel – that's 88%. The second major threat is the United States – that's 77%. Iran is listed as a threat by 10%.

With regard to nuclear weapons, rather remarkably, a majority – in fact, 57% – say that it would have a positive effect in the region if Iran *had* nuclear weapons. Now, these are not small numbers. 88, 77, say the US and Israel are the major threat. 10 say Iran is the major threat. This may not be reported in the newspapers here – it is in England – but it's certainly familiar to the Israeli and US governments, and to the ambassadors. But there is not a word about it anywhere. What that reveals is the profound hatred for democracy on the part of our political leadership and the Israeli political leadership. These things aren't even to be mentioned. This seeps its way all through the diplomatic service. The cables do not have any indication of that.

When they talk about Arabs, they mean the Arab dictators, not the population, which is *overwhelmingly* opposed to the conclusions that the analysts here – Clinton and the media – have drawn. There's also a minor problem; that's the major problem. The minor problem is that we don't know from the cables what the Arab leaders think and say. We know what was selected from the range of what they say. So there is a filtering process. We don't know how much it distorts the information. But there is no question that what is a radical distortion is – or, not even a distortion, a *reflection* – of the concern that the dictators are what matter. The population does not matter, even if it's overwhelmingly opposed to US policy.

There are similar things elsewhere, just keeping to this region. One of the most interesting cables was from the US ambassador in Israel to Hillary Clinton, which described the attack on Gaza – which we should call the US/Israeli attack on Gaza – December 2008. It states correctly there had been a truce. It does not add that during the truce – which was really not observed by Israel – Hamas scrupulously observed it; according to the Israeli government, not a single rocket was fired. That's an omission. But then comes a straight lie: it says that in December 2008, Hamas renewed rocket firing and therefore Israel had to attack in self-defence. Now, the ambassador *surely* is aware, there must be somebody in the American Embassy who reads the Israeli press – the mainstream Israeli press – in which case the embassy is *surely* aware that it is exactly the opposite: Hamas was calling for a renewal of the cease-fire. Israel considered the offer and rejected it, preferring to bomb rather than have security. Also omitted is that while Israel never observed the cease-fire – it maintained the siege in violation of the truce agreement – on November 4, the date of the US election 2008, the Israeli army invaded Gaza, killed half a dozen Hamas militants, which did lead to an exchange of fire in which all the casualties, as usual, were Palestinian. Then in December, when the truce officially ended, Hamas called for renewing it. Israel refused, and the US and Israel chose to launch the war. What the embassy reported is a *gross* falsification and a very significant one since it has to do with the justification for the murderous attack, which means either the embassy hasn't a clue to what is going on or else they're lying outright.

And the latest report that just came out – from Oxfam, from Amnesty International, and other groups – about the effects of the siege on Gaza? What's happening right now?

A siege is an act of war. If anyone insists on that, it is Israel. Israel launched two wars – 1956 and 1967 – in part on grounds its access to the outside world was very partially restricted. That very partial siege they considered an act of war and justification for – one of several justifications

– for what they called 'preventive' or, if you like, pre-emptive war. So they understand that perfectly well, and the point is correct. The siege is a criminal act, in the first place. The Security Council has called on Israel to lift it, and others have. It's designed, as Israeli officials have stated, to keep the people of Gaza to minimal level of existence. They do not want to kill them all off because that would not look good in international opinion. As they put it, 'to keep them on a diet'. This justification began very shortly after the official Israeli withdrawal. There was an election in January 2006; the *only* free election in the Arab world – carefully monitored, recognized to be free – but it had a flaw. The wrong people won. Namely Hamas, which the US did not want and Israel did not want. Instantly, within days, the US and Israel instituted harsh measures to punish the people of Gaza for voting the wrong way in a free election.

The next step was that the US and Israel sought, along with the Palestinian Authority, to try to carry out a military coup in Gaza, to overthrow the elected government. This failed. Hamas beat back the coup attempt. That was July 2007. At that point, the siege got *much* harsher. In between there are many acts of violence, shellings, invasions and so on and so forth. But basically, Israel claims that when the truce was established in summer 2008, Israel's reason for not observing it and withdrawing the siege was that there was an Israeli soldier, Gilad Shalit, who was captured at the border. International commentary regards this as a terrible crime. Well, whatever you think about it, capturing a soldier of an attacking army – and the army was attacking Gaza – capturing a soldier of an attacking army isn't anywhere *near* the level of the crime of kidnapping civilians. Just one day before the capture of Gilad Shalit at the border, Israeli troops had entered Gaza, kidnapped two civilians – the Muammar Brothers – and spirited them across the border. They've disappeared somewhere in Israel's prison system, which is where hundreds, maybe a thousand or so people are sometimes there for years without charges. There are also secret prisons. We don't know what happens there.

This alone is a *far* worse crime than the kidnapping of Shalit. In fact, you could argue there was a reason why it was barely covered: Israel has been doing this for years, in fact, decades. Kidnapping, capturing people, hijacking ships, killing people, bringing them to Israel sometimes as hostages for many years. So this is regular practice; Israel can do what it likes. But the reaction here and the rest of the world regarding the Shalit kidnapping – not kidnapping, you don't *kidnap* soldiers – the *capture* of a soldier as an unspeakable crime, justification for maintaining murders and siege, that's disgraceful.

Noam, so you have Amnesty International, Oxfam, Save the Children, and eighteen other aid groups calling on Israel to unconditionally lift the blockade of Gaza. And you have in the WikiLeaks release a US diplomatic cable, provided to The Guardian *by WikiLeaks, laying out 'National human intelligence collection directive: Asking US personnel to obtain details of travel plans such as routes and vehicles used by Palestinian Authority leaders and Hamas members'. The cable demands 'Biographical, financial, biometric information on key Palestinian Authority and Hamas leaders and representatives to include the Young Guard inside Gaza, the West Bank, and outside,' it says.*

That should not come as much of a surprise. Contrary to the image that is portrayed here, the United States is not an honest broker. It is a participant, a *direct* and *crucial* participant, in Israeli crimes, both in the West Bank and in Gaza. The attack in Gaza was a clear case in point: they used American weapons, the US blocked cease-fire efforts, they gave diplomatic support. The same is true of the daily ongoing crimes in the West Bank, and we should not forget that. Actually, in Area C – the area of the West Bank that Israel controls – conditions for Palestinians have been reported by Save The Children to be worse than in Gaza. Again, this all takes place on the basis of crucial, decisive, US military, diplomatic, and economic support; and also ideological support – meaning, distorting the situation, as is done again, dramatically, in the cables.

The siege itself is simply criminal. It is not only blocking desperately needed aid from coming in, it also drives Palestinians away from the border. Gaza is a small place, heavily and densely overcrowded. And Israeli fire and attacks drive Palestinians away from the Arab land on the border, and also drive fishermen in from Gaza into territorial waters. They are compelled by Israeli gunboats – all illegal, of course – to fish right near the shore where fishing is almost impossible because Israel has destroyed the power systems and sewage systems and the contamination is terrible. This is just a stranglehold to punish people for being there and for insisting on voting the wrong way. Israel decided, 'We don't want this anymore. Let's just get rid of them'.

We should also remember that US/Israeli policy since Oslo, since the early 1990s, has been to separate Gaza from the West Bank. That is in straight violation of the Oslo agreements, but it has been carried out systematically, and it has a big effect. It means almost half the Palestinian population would be cut off from any possible political arrangement that would be made. It also means Palestine loses its access to the outside world. Gaza *should* have and *can* have airports and seaports. Right now, Israel has taken over about 40% of the West Bank. Obama's latest offers have granted even more, and they're certainly planning to take more. What is left is just cantonized. It's what the planner, Ariel Sharon, called Bantustans. And they're in prison, too, as Israel takes over the Jordan Valley and drives Palestinians out. So these are all crimes of a piece.

The Gaza siege is particularly grotesque because of the conditions under which people are forced to live. I mean, if a young person in Gaza, a student in Gaza, let's say, wants to study in a West Bank university, they can't do it. If a person in Gaza needs advanced medical treatment from an East Jerusalem hospital where the treatment is available, they can't go! Medicines are held back. It is a scandalous crime, all around.

What do you think the United States should do in this case?

What the United States should do is very simple: it should join the world. I mean, there are negotiations going on, supposedly. As they are presented here, the standard picture is that the US is an honest broker trying to bring together two recalcitrant opponents – Israel and Palestinian Authority. That's just a charade.

If there were serious negotiations, they would be organized by some neutral party and the US and Israel would be on one side and the world would be on the other side. And that is not an exaggeration. It should not be a secret that there has long been an overwhelming international consensus on a diplomatic, political solution. Everyone knows the basic outlines; some of the details you can argue about. It includes everyone except the United States and Israel. The US has been blocking it for 35 years with occasional departures brief ones. It includes the Arab League. It includes the Organization of Islamic States, which happens to include Iran. It includes every relevant actor except the United States and Israel, the two rejectionist states. So, if there were to be negotiations that were serious, that's the way they would be organized. The actual negotiations barely reach the level of comedy. The issue that's being debated is a footnote, a *minor* footnote: expansion of settlements. Of course it's illegal. In fact, everything Israel is doing in the West Bank and Gaza is illegal. That hasn't even been controversial since 1967.

With grateful acknowledgements to Noam Chomsky and democracynow.org, who licensed the original content of this program under a Creative Commons Licence.

America's shiver

Paul Rogers

We first wrote about Full Spectrum Dominance back in 2001, before 9/11 (see Spokesman 71, *entitled* Full Spectrum Absurdity*). Ten years on, that mindset apparently persists amongst certain circles in the United States, as some of the leaked diplomatic cables indicate. Paul Rogers sifts the evidence. Professor Rogers' book,* Losing Control: Global Security in the 21st Century, *is now in its third edition (Pluto Press).*

The hacked United States diplomatic missives reveal both the vast ambition and the new vulnerabilites of the world's superpower.

Among the most compelling nuggets of information contained in the batch of United States diplomatic documents released by WikiLeaks, and published in leading international newspapers, is the list of installations in more than fifty countries which the State Department in Washington deems to be a US security concern. Some of the locations seem obvious (major oil-and-gas processing-plants and pipeline terminuses, for example); but others are far harder to fit any evident national-security frame (such as an Australian pharmaceutical plant specialising in anti-snake-venom treatments, and cobalt mines in the Democratic Republic of Congo).

But even the more unlikely sites are relevant to a country that sees itself as the world's sole superpower with interests across the globe. The anti-snake-venom plant in Australia almost certainly has the expertise and equipment to make antidotes to other toxins, and this could be highly significant in the event of a biological-warfare threat.

The cobalt-mines around Kolwezi and Mutshatsha in the southern DRC extract the world's most important deposits of cobalt ores, and ferro-alloys containing cobalt have the specific property of retaining their shape at very high temperatures. They are therefore much in demand for the guidance-vanes of missile-engines and other elements of modern weapons-systems.

The more surprising elements of the list as much as the expected ones thus illustrate the continued reach of the United States' strategic and security ambitions. But they also reveal something more: its new vulnerabilities. The increased inter-state competition across much of the global south from China and other rising states is one, familiar, source of these; another and perhaps less visible source is the challenge posed by insurgent groups to these prime targets. Indeed, central Africa may be a good place to begin to track this superpower dilemma.

A wider trend

In 1977-78, this region of what was then Zaire – ruled by the authoritarian (and west-supported) Mobutu Seso Soko – was a scene of severe violence as forces of the central government in Kinshasa fought to prevent rebel groups taking control of the mines. The insurgents were supported from Soviet bloc countries, especially East Germany, making this also one of the characteristic proxy wars of the Cold-War era. The crisis became so serious that Franco-Belgian paratroopers (supported by Nato) were airlifted to the region to take control of the mines; the contingent, having secured the objective, then handed over to a French-organised Inter-African Force.

Such armed competition over mineral resources both extended beyond the Cold War and acquired new dimensions – among them the capacity and will of paramilitary groups to target sites of great economic value or symbolism to the power-structures they seek to undermine.

In Sri Lanka, for example, the Tamil Tigers guerrilla group attacked an oil refinery, the international airport and many other such sites in the 1990s; its biggest operation was a massive truck-bombing of Colombo's central bank, in January 1996, that killed over 100 people and injured 1,400 as well as damaging both much of the capital's business district and business confidence overall.

A further significant example in this decade is the Provisional IRA's decision to switch the focus of its armed campaign in the early 1990s in the direction of a full-tilt assault against the City of London, at the very time when the latter was competing vigorously with Frankfurt to be Europe's financial hub. A series of bombs in the heart of the extended district – in Bishopsgate, Baltic Exchange and Canary Wharf – was the result; there were also numerous attacks on transport targets including rail terminuses, motorways and airports. The government of the day, led by John Major as Prime Minister (1990-97), never publicly acknowledged the full impact of the IRA's strategic shift; but at the centre of power there was clear recognition of the serious dangers of such 'spectaculars'. The result was to fuel the development of an incipient 'peace process' in Northern Ireland involving all leading actors, initially by Major's Conservative Government but with more focus when Tony Blair's New Labour came to power in May 2007.

The completion of this process, in the form of the Belfast Agreement of 1998, and subsequent events (albeit breakaway or 'dissident' factions claiming the IRA mantle persist in efforts to continue the struggle) took place just as the arc of insurgency was rising elsewhere. In the 2000s, the age of 'war on terror', this form of economic conflict has become part of the armoury of al Qaeda and its affiliates; examples include the attack on the French tanker *Limburg* off the coast of Yemen, on 6 October 2002, and the bombing of the Saudi oil-processing plant at Abqaiq, on 24 February 2006. At the height of the Iraq insurgency, in 2004-07, repeated attacks on oil facilities sabotaged US efforts to develop this asset and to establish control over the country.

There are other cases across the world, perpetrated by groups (such as India's Naxalites) with a quite different ideological character and political motive. A series of low-cost but high-impact attacks on Mexico's oil-and-gas pipelines by the small but effective *Ejército Popular Revolucionario* (Popular Revolutionary Army / EJR), in 2007, would also come into this category.

A real grasp

The wider trend evident here since the 1990s is the ability of paramilitary groups in different parts of the world to recognise the weak points of organised commercial and financial operations and, on many occasions, to target them. These disparate groups are not themselves coordinated or supportive of a single cause, but the body of experience they have separately developed (much of which can be widely accessed and shared across the internet) means that a common understanding of the vulnerabilities of urban-industrial societies is possible.

This trend, and its wider political context, helps explain the desire of the United States State Department to collect data on potential strategic targets in more than fifty countries. The US has faced many problems in the decade of 'war on terror', and its overriding focus on military combat has, in addition, handicapped its ability to cope with emerging issues such as the rise of China as a major economic power. Yet the inner nexus of power in Washington maintains an unbending commitment to the idea of the 'new American century', and the status of the United States as the world's only military superpower.

Жорес Медведев, Рой Медведев

1925—2010

ИЗ ВОСПОМИНАНИЙ

This ambition is manifested in the effort to secure 'full-spectrum dominance' using conventional military forces; the attempt to exert control of space through US Space Command's *Vision for 2020;* and a capacity to project power far in excess of any other state. For all its extraordinary strength and scale, however, the project is as yet unable to prevent sub-state actors from launching damaging assaults and thus maximising the benefits of 'asymmetrical war'.

The insurgencies in Iraq and Afghanistan have already hugely constrained American forces and their coalition partners; both conflicts, too, have elements of an inter-state resource war of the kind familiar from the Cold War period. But in addition to such 'classic' geopolitical and geo-strategic concerns, the United States now faces a further deep underlying worry: that paramilitary groups worldwide are ever more aware that their most effective impact might come less from laying improvised-explosive devices (IEDs) to disable small military units than by striking laterally at major nodes of economic activity.

This process may still be in its early stages. But that is precisely the importance of the diplomatic list of security-related sites released by Wikileaks. The United States, *the* world power, has interests everywhere – and in the new conditions of global politics, conflict, and technology, these are everywhere shadowed by new vulnerabilities. The cables show that Hillary Clinton's State Department has a real grasp of this reality. How the United States responds to it will help define the character of the next decade and beyond.

This article is published by Paul Rogers and openDemocracy.net under a Creative Commons Licence. It is reprinted here with grateful acknowledgements.

Dangerous Occupation

Zhores Medvedev

In November 2010, a volume of memoirs was published in Moscow to mark the 85th birthdays of Roy and Zhores Medvedev. The cover is shown on the facing page. The Medvedev twins have lived through, and sought to explain, some of the most tumultuous developments of modern times. Here, in the first of two parts from this anniversary volume, Zhores recalls how, in 1943, he was called up to fight, was wounded at the front, and later, after some recuperation, began his pursuit of a lifelong career in science.

My family first encountered the war in Rostov-on-Don when I was 15-years-old. Within three months the German army had captured Taganrog, only a hundred kilometres from Rostov. Abandoning everything, we left for Tbilisi, the city where I was born. When the summons arrived from the military recruitment office, with the order to report with my possessions and documents on 1st February 1943, I was still studying in the tenth grade and had only recently turned seventeen. The war was already changing, with the Soviet army liberating the North Caucuses, and drawing nearer to Krasnodar. The army was in urgent need of reinforcements and to this end the period of conscription was shifted; the lower limit by one year and the upper by two years. Young recruits were sent to Kutaisi for training. Here, on the outskirts of the city, was the territory of the reserve regiment, where accelerated military training in shooting, throwing hand-grenades, *plastun* crawling [flat on the ground for scouting purposes], using a bayonet, pistol-whipping and handling an entrenching tool took place. I was assigned to our conscription's first infantry company, who were sent to the field at the end of April. The military echelon advanced from Kutaisi to Krasnodar through Baku and the recently liberated North Caucuses. Local residents at the train stations would bring us milk and bread, sometimes lard as well. From Krasnodar we arrived in cars to the Krymskaya *stanitsa* [Cossack village] on the Taman Peninsular. This *stanitsa* was liberated only a week earlier during battles to breach the 'blue line' of the German army that was protecting the outskirts of

Novorossiysk and Kerch. The landing force was deployed by sea, not far from Novorossiysk, which pushed the Germans back and created a bridgehead: this was the famous *Malaya Zemlya*. According to the plan of the command – which was explained to us after we were conscripted to the 169th infantry regiment – our regiment was to be part of the force used to break through the second boundary of the 'blue line', and liberate the Kievskaya *stanitsa*. Powerful technology, including Katusha rocket launchers, had been assembled to support the infantry (mostly artillery), with no less than two hundred barrels along each kilometre of the front. Infantry units, upon breaking through the German defence, were to take the next frontier 'on the shoulders of the retreating enemy', by order of the command. The German army had many fortified sites on the outskirts of Novorossiysk.

Military operations on the Taman Peninsular are almost unheard of in western literature on the history of the war, but the concentration of troops here was no less than on other fronts. The 17th regular German army, which had sixteen infantry divisions – two armoured and four separate regiments – was deployed on the front line, stretching for just less than a hundred kilometres. From the Crimea, the German army was protected by more than a thousand aeroplanes, amounting to almost as many troops and as much equipment as there had been in the army of Field Marshall Paulus at Stalingrad. There were three armies on the Soviet side of the Taman Peninsular, consisting of twenty-one divisions and five independent brigades. Thirty kilometres ahead of the 56th army, which was commanded by General Grechko, stood five divisions of the German army in a deep defensive line. The breaching of the German defences was relatively quick following air strikes and a vigorous artillery barrage. Barbed wire fencing was scattered along the sides. Soldiers walked in several rows through the German trenches. Holding our rifles with fixed bayonets at the ready, we ran, mostly over the corpses of German soldiers. Anti-personnel mines were the main problem on approaches to the trenches; they were everywhere, with no less than a thousand on each kilometre of the front line. We approached the German trenches in rows, one after the other. Whoever was in front often trod on a mine …

Beyond the German positions was a very hilly steppe. The green gardens of Kievskaya *stanitsa* were already visible in the distance. But ahead of this, another multi-layered German defence line, complete with barbed wire and minefields, had been built earlier. Our regiment wasn't able to take the enemy in its stride since the enemy didn't retreat, and instead fired their machine guns. We took cover and started to dig. I was lucky as there was a crater nearby caused by a bomb, which I quickly turned into a deep trench. It started going dark. In the darkness the company's horse-drawn field kitchen arrived, bringing bread, tobacco, sugar and bottles of vodka. During combat every soldier relied on his famous 'hundred grams from the People's Commissar'. Mess tins were filled with hot food. Millet porridge with American tinned meat. But only a small queue lined up for the company kitchen. In the woods earlier that day, before the start of the breach, there were 150 riflemen in the company commanded by Captain Petrov. It had been at full-strength. By evening on the first day of fighting thirty men remained in the ranks. After food, ammunition was brought to us. I took a box of cartridges and six grenades. The other soldiers also stocked up for a long time.

The following day the Germans suddenly launched a counter-attack. Their generals knew that sparse units in disordered individual trenches stood opposite their lines. It is difficult to manage this kind of defence as every soldier acts individually. The main counter-strike was aimed at a nearby regiment. We were further up, they were below, around 400-500 metres from our positions. About twenty German tanks were seen crawling away in the distance with small figurines of soldiers behind them. A second lieutenant came running from the regiment staff and gave the order to 'support neighbours with fire'. After that he did not return to the staff dug-out, but jumped down into my trench. I had enough room for two. Aiming fire on fleeing German soldiers at such a distance was impossible. But I was shooting in the direction of the tanks, quickly changing clip for clip. I had a lot of cartridges. The second lieutenant all of a sudden asked me to let him shoot, so I gave him the rifle and sat down to rest. He leaned out, took aim, but did not manage to fire. There was some sort of gurgling sound and my neighbour started sliding down. He was dead; a bullet had pierced his neck. Before standing up I got my helmet stuck on my bayonet. Ding! The helmet was pierced right through. Soviet helmets were too thin. They defended us only from fragments of mines and grenades. Somewhere near our positions a German sniper held us in his sights.

The counter-attacks were repelled. Individual trenches did not give room for manoeuvre, but nobody ran from them in the open steppe. We needed to fight until the end. Every soldier there had a lot of cartridges and grenades. Three German tanks remained on the battlefield. At night the soldiers of a neighbouring regiment were taken to the rear, having been replaced by a reserve battalion. Many were carried away on stretchers.

Over the next few days the German sniper increased the number of our losses. Individual trenches severely limited the opportunities for active defence. Olya – a young female signaller providing telephone communication between the company commander and the battalion commander – was killed by mortar fire during the next attempt to restore the faulty wire, which stretched across the ground to the rear defences. They appointed me as a signaller. The first two missions – to restore communications – I carried out in darkness. It was relatively safe. Taking the telephone cable under my arm and the coil of insulation tape in my hands, I had to go to the rear defences. Having found the gaps in the wire, it was necessary to smooth out the ends, join them up and insulate them with the tape. On the whole line for a kilometre up to the battalion dug-out there could have been five or six gaps. On 31st May, after the early morning air bombardment which damaged the telephone wires again, Popov ordered me to quickly restore communications. Seizing the wire and dropping low, I ran to the rear defences. The first gap was around twenty metres from our positions and I hurriedly re-connected it. But, leaping into the next run, I felt a heavy blow on my right foot which was already elevated above the ground. I fell and quickly began to crawl back, understanding I was wounded. In the company medical trench two nurses dressed the open wound which had almost stopped bleeding. The blood only started flowing again when I crawled to my trench. I bandaged my leg, but wasn't able to stop the bleeding. What happened next I can't remember. I only regained consciousness the following morning after a blood transfusion in the field hospital. Casualties were only removed from their positions at night.

Biology, medicine or agronomics?

In January 1944 I came to Moscow from Rostov-on-Don with the intention of entering the faculty of biology at MGU (Moscow State University). Students were not accepted in the winter, but I had no other way out. In December 1943 the bones in my foot, fragmented by a bullet on the Taman Peninsular, had healed well enough to permit me to replace my crutches with a walking stick. Following the injury I visited three military hospitals, first in Krasnodar, after that in Baku and then in Tbilisi, my hometown. There was so large a flow of casualties from the Taman front in summer 1943 that all the hospitals in Transcaucasia were overcrowded. To suddenly find myself in Tbilisi was a great stroke of luck. My mother knew nothing of my fate for almost three months. My brother, Roy, was on military service as a non-combatant. As a soldier discharged with a disability, I now had the right to return to Rostov, which had been liberated in the spring of 1943. Decrees had been enacted which granted returnees to liberated cities the right to accommodation.

Rostov-on-Don, which was twice occupied in autumn 1941 and summer 1942, had endured heavy bombing. But the five-floor house at 78 Pushkin Street, where our two-roomed flat was, had not been damaged. The flat belonged to our aunt, Nadya, and our grandmother. We came to them after the arrest of our father, Aleksandr Romanovich, a professor of the military academy, in August 1938. He was convicted as a 'Bukharinist' and died, in March 1941, in one of the camps in the Magadan oblast. Father was a very strong man and he physically toughened both my brother and I from early childhood. But he did not survive his job in the copper mines of Kolyma. There were now three families living together in our apartment in Rostov; they had been resettled from destroyed houses. It made no sense to plead for its return. Things that belonged to us were no longer there. Our father's large book collection, which we valued the most, had disappeared. Having not left the city, my great aunt, a well-known dentist in Rostov with her own office on the main Budennii Prospect, was executed together with her husband as part of the liquidation of all Rostov's Jews by the Germans. The second occupation of Rostov occurred from 24th July 1942, but as early as 11th-12th August, all the Jews remaining in the city – around 15,000 people, including children – were executed at the Zmievskaya gorge outside the city.

We tried to persuade our aunt to leave but she didn't want to abandon everything, placing hopes instead on her Russian surname 'Sakharova', and on the need for good dentists under any regime. She had no children of her own. An officer of the Gestapo moved into her splendid apartment during the occupation. Some other families also lived there now. I spent about a week in Rostov. I was given shelter by the mother of my friend from school, Kostya Ragozin, who had been fighting somewhere in Belarus. His father 'went missing' in summer 1942 on the outskirts of Stalingrad. There was nothing for me to do in the city, so I went to the train station to go to Moscow. At that time every passenger train had a carriage 'for the wounded', in which, dressed in a soldier's overcoat, it was possible to travel without tickets. The carriage was very crowded. There was still no direct connection between Rostov and Moscow and the train passed through the ruins of Stalingrad. I only turned up in Moscow six days later. On the road at the stations there were special canteens for discharged soldiers returning from hospitals. A quarter of the passengers in the carriage were serious cases, quite often with amputated legs – orderlies or nurses accompanying them.

The dean of the faculty of biology cordially welcomed me and was prepared to enrol me to commence studies in October. At the time disabled veterans were accepted into higher education institutions under special conditions and without entrance examinations. There were very few male students. But the university, having only recently re-opened since the evacuation to Kazan, still had no students' hostels. They had the same problems in the medical institute with student halls. My erudition in the problems of medicine obviously surprised the director of the institute (based on the books of Mechnikov, Paul de Kruif and Bogomolets, which I had read in Rostov). He was prepared to accept me as a student immediately, but only in the faculty of hygiene. 'You skipped human anatomy. Without that there's nothing you can do in the faculty of medicine. You'll have to wait until autumn.'

I had lived in Moscow for five days, spending my nights at either the Kazansky or Leningradsky rail terminals. Under the rationing system it was only possible to buy food at train stations in the separate halls for servicemen and those discharged from the army. Here and there were also canteens for the wounded. Hundreds of thousands of disabled veterans, discharged from hospitals, travelled across the country, without the possibility of returning home. The authorities simply did not know what to do with them, and rail terminals became communal living areas for these people. Their hometowns and villages were badly, and often completely, ruined or not yet liberated. In January 1944 the Crimea and Odessa were still occupied by the German army; the fight for the city of Krivoi Rog was ongoing. At the same time the German armies surrounding Leningrad suffered a crushing defeat. All of Belarus, the Baltic countries and Moldova had yet to be liberated.

I arrived at the Petrovsko-Razumovskoe platform at the Moscow North suburb on the commuter train from the Leningradsky rail terminal. Sprawled out over a large area were the beautiful academic buildings, halls of residence, experimental fields, ponds and woods of the Moscow Agricultural Academy, named after K.A. Timiryazev. The dean of the faculty of agronomy, Professor Nikolai Aleksandrovich Maisuryan, turned out to be my compatriot; he was born and graduated from university in Tbilisi. I was again invited to apply to become a student in the autumn. Before the start of the new academic year I was also offered work and residence. The work was simple but dangerous, washing white quartz sand with hydrochloric acid to clear all the mineral salts from it. You had to put on a gas mask in the basement where the wash tanks were. This sand, having been cleaned with both hydrochloric acid and distilled water, was then used by the ton in agro-chemical and physiological experiments with different combinations of fertilisers. In spring, as a worker at the experiment station, I was offered two hundred square metres of a ploughed field at the Otradnoe experimental farm. In October, when I finally became a student, two large sacks of potatoes lay under my bed in the room I shared with three other students.

Trofim Denisovich Lysenko

My interests in the problems of ageing arose when I was 15 or 16 years old. In the winter of 1942 I sat for hours in the Tbilisi public library summarising A.V. Nagornii's monograph, 'The problem of ageing and longevity', published in Kharkov in 1940 with a total circulation of 400 copies. In the agricultural academy were the departments of zoology, botany, chemistry and physical chemistry, physiology and biochemistry. The fact that this applied to plants and animals rather than humans did not matter. Plants and animals grow old, too, albeit unequally. Weismann's theory on the mortality of soma and the immortality of germ plasma explains the necessity of ageing of the body for animals logically enough. But plants obviously do not have the germ lines separate from soma. They were capable of unlimited vegetative reproduction. It was possible to get a new plant from somatic cells. Plants were reproduced by tubers, grafts and root sprays. The growing point of the stem, consisting of rapidly dividing vegetative cells which formed leaves unexpectedly in spring, summer or, in warmer regions, autumn, and sometimes even throughout the year, suddenly began to form a flower with a full set of male and female reproductive organs. The first theory I developed tried to explain this problem. I assumed that in the growing points of plants there are, potentially, also stem or germ cells amongst somatic cells. Somatic cells, reducing their cell division because of ageing, gradually become mixed up with embryonic stem cells and the growing point does not begin to form leaves, but rather a flower with sexual organs. Sometimes this deceleration of cell division in somatic programmed cells can be caused by cold temperature, as in winter plants. My theory on this embellishes the theory of the developmental stages of plants, which made Trofim Lysenko famous back in 1929, when, for the first time in practice, he was able to bring winter wheat to reproduction during the spring sowing, having kept sprouted grain for two weeks under melting snow. I committed my theory to a five-page manuscript in calligraphic handwriting and sent a copy, in April 1945, to Academician Lysenko, president of the Lenin All-Union Academy of Agricultural Sciences (LAAAS). I passed another copy on to the head of the department of botany at our academy (TAA), Professor Petr

Mikhailovich Zhukovsky, whose lectures for us as first year students were most enjoyable. Two weeks later I received a reply in an envelope from LAAAS. The letter from Lysenko was short: 'Dear Zhores Aleksandrovich! Your ideas seem interesting to me. Drop by if you're in Moscow. Academician, T.D. Lysenko'.

The Lenin Academy, on Bolshoi Kharitonyevskoi Lane in the centre of Moscow, occupied the ancient palace of the Yupusov princes. A plaque on one side of the entrance informed that it was a monument of seventeenth-century architecture, protected by the state. Around thirty people were already sitting in the spacious reception room in front of the doors to the president's office. The secretary and assistant greeted the new arrivals, asking their reasons for visiting. I showed the assistant my letter. Lysenko began receiving guests at 11 o'clock. We were told that the academician did not accept guests in turn, but everyone at once. He started to talk at first with an agronomist who had come from Siberia. We were able to sit in the office and could ask questions and make comments. Quite often, as we were told, people come to the academician with exactly the same problems. There are no restrictions on entry. Interesting thoughts often come to the academician during the course of these conversations.

At precisely 11 o'clock visitors began to enter the president's large office. Lysenko was already sitting behind his huge desk. He had entered through a separate door. Offices of important Soviet administrators always consisted of two rooms: one large for receptions, and a second 'personal' room with a sofa-bed for relaxing, a sideboard and lavatory. Lysenko's table was full of agricultural products; a few small sheaves of wheat and rye, big potatoes and corns on the cob. The large wheat sheaves, brought from all over the country, stood near the walls next to the writing table. Chairs for the visitors took up positions along the side walls. Bookcases, which are always found in the offices of deans, directors and professors, were not visible. 'Take a seat', Lysenko called to us in a surprisingly loud but very hoarse voice. 'I will speak with the agronomist from the Omsk oblast [he called out the surname]. He has a question concerning the sowing of winter wheat crops.' In 1943-44 the sowing of winter wheat crops in the harvest field by Lysenko's method – that is, on untreated rather than ploughed fields – was the main topic of discussion in agricultural circles. In 1942 the German army offensive on the North Caucuses and Stalingrad only started at the end of July, when the harvesting of winter wheat had already been completed. A large amount of grain was rescued in Transcaucasia and across the Volga, but the sowing of winter wheat for the harvest in 1943 could not be carried out anywhere. Winter wheat was not sown in Siberia as the region was too cold. Lysenko had proposed to sow winter wheat in the Omsk and Novosibirsk oblasts in unploughed fields. According to his theory, which there was no time to check, the death of shoots in winter is not caused by frost, but from the formation of ice crystals and the compression and movement of the freezing loose earth, tearing the nodes of cereal grass and roots under the ground. On dense, unploughed land there would be no such gaps and shoots would not be lost. If the nodes remained intact, plants would regenerate their lateral buds and all their shoots in the spring. The stubble remaining from the harvested crops preserves the snow better, protecting the soil. In August-September 1942 in the Chelyabinsk, Novosibirsk and Omsk oblasts hundreds of thousands of hectares were sown on the harvest fields. The results were contradictory. Some collective farms had harvests; on others the crops were lost. The agronomist from Siberia was one of those for whom the harvest suffered. They mustered: how many have sown? The debate started. Those seated along the wall actively took part. At around one o'clock the waitresses entered the office with trays, serving the seated visitors strong tea in glasses with silver glass-holders and big sandwiches with red caviar and salmon. It was a pleasant surprise. By 3 o'clock the reception had ended – Lysenko said he was expected in the Kremlin for a conference. I did not get to discuss my theory, but I returned to the student halls fully satisfied.

Petr Mikhailovich Zhukovsky

Professor Zhukovsky was one of the most popular and influential teachers in our academy. He was an academician of LAAAS, laureate of the State Stalin Prize, and the author of what was considered to be the best botany textbook. He collected thousands of samples of cultivated plants during expeditions to Asia Minor, Syria and Mesopotamia, wrote the book *Agricultural Turkey*, and discovered a new species in the Caucuses – a previously unknown wheat, unique in its high immunity to fungal diseases. This species of wheat, named by Zhukovsky as *Tritium Timopheev Zhuk* (in honour of his teacher, Timofeev), was used for hybridisation by wheat breeders in many countries to strengthen the immunity of their output.

Zhukovsky did not need to respond to my letter. Botany was one of the main first year subjects and our study group came to the department of botany in block 17 every week for practical work. Out of twenty group members I was the only male and Zhukovsky already knew me. After a regular seminar I was told that Petr Mikhailovich was waiting for me in his office. Zhukovsky greeted me cordially, warm-heartedly even. The laboratory assistant brought us tea and cheese sandwiches. Zhukovsky praised my writing and style: 'Your manuscript is written in good scientific language'. He asked me a little about myself. 'My son, Alesha, is now at the front too, already in Germany. I hope he is ok.' (At that time, at the end of April, fighting was going on in Berlin). 'Let's test your theory together. We have a laboratory of embryology and cell biology in our department. We'll give you a good microscope. But you need to learn a lot …' The following day I went to the laboratory. It was managed by Anaida Iosifovna Atabekova, an experienced cell biologist and lecturer. As it turned out, she was the wife of the dean, Maisuryan, and was also born in Tbilisi.

Two weeks later the war ended. Zhukovsky's son, Aleksei, survived and I met him the following year. My friend from Rostov, Kostya Ragozin, was killed during the street battles in Berlin. I learned of this from his mother when I visited the city again in 1946.

To be continued.

Translated by Andrew Ramsbottom with additional editing by Sarah O'Malley.

*   *   *

Select Bibliography
Zhores Medvedev has a long list of works to his name. They have been
   translated into many languages. Those published in English include:
The Rise and Fall of T. D. Lysenko (Columbia University Press, 1969)
Question of Madness, with Roy Medvedev (Macmillan, 1971)
Ten Years after Ivan Denisovich (Macmillan, 1973)
Khrushchev: The Years in Power, with Roy Medvedev (Columbia
   University Press, 1976)
Soviet Science (Oxford University Press, 1978)
Nuclear Disaster in the Urals (W.W.Norton, 1979)
Andropov: His Life and Death (Blackwell, 1984)
Soviet Agriculture (W.W. Norton, 1987)
Gorbachev (Blackwell, 1987)
The Legacy of Chernobyl (Blackwell, 1990)
The Unknown Stalin, with Roy Medvedev (IB Tauris, 2003)

Love of learning

Students lead the way

Jeremy Corbyn MP

Jeremy Corbyn is Labour MP for Islington North. He has contributed a foreword to Spokesman's new edition of J.A. Hobson' classic Imperialism *(£19.95 spokesmanbooks.com).*

Helmeted riot police, shields and batons drawn, welcomed the education protesters in Whitehall in December and ushered them into an immediate kettle. The same picture was mirrored in Parliament Square and Embankment where the National Union of Students (NUS) and University and College Union (UCU) had hoped to rally to express their disdain.

Six hours later, the students and their unaffiliated supporters emerged shocked, distressed, exhausted and entirely unempowered in the decision-making process which will determine their future and those of their children – if they can afford to have them.

From the comfort of the House of Commons, Business Secretary Vince Cable – having turned from economic saint to monetarist ogre in seven months – calmly told the house that state support for higher education teaching would reduce from 60 per cent to 40, and that the rest would be 'made up by the private sector'. This actually amounts to wholesale privatisation and an increasing loss of academic independence. And in the case of arts and humanities, the cut is 100 per cent – effectively closing those courses to ordinary people.

The last decade has seen increased access to higher education and a much more socially and ethnically diverse student population. Tens of thousands of those among the current student population are the first of their family ever to get to university. Tragically they could be the last. Access to universities is not just determined by the level of fees but also by enabling 16-year-olds to stay on at school or college.

This has been made possible mainly because of the education maintenance allowance (EMA), which has given students some limited support on the road to university. The Coalition Government now plans to take this away too, removing the opportunity for the next generation to have a chance of even getting to the foothills of a university course.

A 2008 National Union of Students' survey of 1,205 EMA recipients – conducted four years after its introduction – showed that 61 per cent felt they would have been unable to continue without it. This was when the banking crisis was encouraging 'thinking the unthinkable'. To its credit the Labour government maintained the payment. In the run-up to the 2010 election, nobody said they would abolish it – indeed the Tories specifically said they would keep it.

The Coalition Government's massively unpopular decisions will force the next generation of students to either walk into crippling debt or to not pursue higher education at all.

The last time this issue was voted on, in 2004, the Tories and Lib Dems voted against raising fees to £3,000. On that occasion – and on the first introduction of fees in 1998 – Labour left MPs voted against it. In December 2010, all Labour MPs voted against. The only consistency in all this has been among those who believe in fee-free higher education.

There is a pattern to the Con-Dem plans for education, which will take Britain back to the 1950s. They constantly assert that 'we are all in this together', and at the same time make the largest cuts on the most socially useful areas of spending such as support for higher education, keeping students in school, or helping them into work through the Future Jobs Fund. On top of this, the huge cuts in local government spending will cost jobs, deepen the recession and throw the floodgates open for reckless privatisation.

We need look only to Greece and Ireland for confirmation of where this leads. And, as in Greece, the actions of tens of thousands of students have changed the face of British politics.

The optimism and determination of the current generation to make sure the next has the same opportunities is an inspiration. In the first student demonstration the police and Parliament's authorities were surprised by the numbers. In the second there was the introduction of kettling and, in December, 3,000 police were deployed to 'control' the outcry. In Parliament, coalition MPs indulged in an orgy of self-righteous indignation about the problems of disorder that followed. Only a few MPs touched on the highly questionable tactics of imprisoning students and children on the streets without charge for many hours. Home Secretary

Theresa May claimed that anyone was able to leave the cordon if they wished, while outside the reality-distortion bubble of Parliament many were forced to spend a freezing afternoon on the streets, unable to get anywhere near to lobbying their MPs.

Labour's Dennis Skinner pointed out forcefully to May that, after only a short time in power, the government had already deployed vast numbers of police to try to suppress protest, creating scenes starkly reminiscent of the poll tax demonstrations 20 years ago, or the miners' marches five years before that.

The Lib Dems, having campaigned so assiduously for the votes of students and their parents by promising the abolition of fees altogether, have suffered the biggest backlash. However, we should not forget that it is a Tory-led government. The mean-spirited, divisive and uncaring attitudes of Thatcherite Britain are coming back. While the education vote resulted in a coalition majority, it was a hollow victory. The education protests are far from over.

The coming battle over educational maintenance allowance will bring more unrest, the weight of which will be bolstered by others equally determined to defend public services such as post offices or hospitals. Cuts are unnecessary and the attack on services and public employment is nothing less than vindictive and brutal. It is now up to the Labour Party to learn the lessons of the election defeat and develop policies that maintain full employment and the welfare state. This means that the yawning gap between the richest and the rest has to be addressed and wealth must be redistributed. The whole labour movement is obliged now to reconnect with its history and remember the need to speak out for basic principles.

Our young protesters are leading the way.

NATO in US Grand Strategy

Diana Johnstone

Diana Johnstone is the author of Fools Crusade: Yugoslavia, NATO and Western Delusions *(Pluto Press, £17.99) and, with Jean Bricmont, of* Humanitarian Imperialism: Using Human Rights to Sell War *(Monthly Review Press, £15.95).*

On 19 and 20 November 2010, NATO leaders met in Lisbon for what was billed as a summit on 'NATO's Strategic Concept'. Among topics of discussion was an array of scary 'threats', from cyber-war to climate change, as well as nice protective things such as nuclear weapons and a high-tech, Maginot Line boondoggle supposed to stop enemy missiles in mid-air. The NATO leaders were unable to avoid talking about the war in Afghanistan, that endless crusade which unites the civilized world against the elusive Old Man of the Mountain, Hassan i Sabah, eleventh century chief of the Assassins, in his latest reincarnation as Osama bin Laden. There will, no doubt, be much talk of 'our shared values'.

Most of what they discussed is fiction with a price tag. The one thing missing from the Strategic Concept summit agenda was a serious discussion of strategy. This is partly because NATO, as such, has no strategy, and cannot have its own strategy. NATO is, in reality, an instrument of United States' strategy. Its only operative Strategic Concept is the one put into practice by the United States. But even that is an elusive phantom. American leaders seem to prefer striking postures, 'showing resolve', to defining strategies.

One who does presume to define strategy is Zbigniew Brzezinski, godfather of the Afghan Mujahideen back when they could be used to destroy the Soviet Union. Brzezinski was not shy about bluntly stating the strategic objective of US policy in his 1993 book *The Grand Chessboard*: 'American primacy'. As for NATO, he described it as one of the institutions serving to perpetuate American hegemony, 'making the United States a key participant even in intra-European affairs'. In its 'global web of specialized institutions', which of course includes NATO, the United States exercises power through 'continuous bargaining, dialogue, diffusion, and quest for formal consensus, even though that power originates ultimately from a single source, namely, Washington, DC'.

The description perfectly fits the Lisbon 'Strategic Concept' conference. Before the conference, NATO's Danish secretary general, Anders Fogh Rasmussen, announced that 'we are pretty close to a consensus'. And this consensus, according to the *New York Times*, 'will probably follow President Barack Obama's own formulation: to work toward a non-nuclear world while maintaining a nuclear deterrent'.

Wait a minute, does that make sense? No, but it is the stuff of NATO consensus. Peace through war, nuclear disarmament through nuclear armament, and above all, defense of member states by sending expeditionary forces to infuriate the natives of distant lands.

A strategy is not a consensus written by committees.

The American method of 'continuous bargaining, dialogue, diffusion, and quest for formal consensus' wears down whatever resistance may occasionally appear. Thus, Germany and France initially resisted Georgian membership in NATO, as well as the notorious 'missile shield', both seen as blatant provocations, apt to set off a new arms race with Russia, and damage fruitful German and French relations with Moscow, for no useful purpose. But the United States does not take 'no' for an answer, and keeps repeating its imperatives until resistance fades. The one recent exception was the French refusal to join the invasion of Iraq, but the angry US reaction scared the conservative French political class into supporting the pro-American Nicolas Sarkozy.

In search of 'threats' and 'challenges'

The very heart of what passes for a 'strategic concept' was first declared and put into operation in the spring of 1999, when NATO defied international law, the United Nations and its own original charter by waging an aggressive war outside its defensive perimeter against Yugoslavia. That transformed NATO from a defensive to an offensive alliance. Ten years later, the godmother of that war, Madeleine Albright, was picked to chair the 'group of experts' that spent several months holding seminars, consultations and meetings preparing the Lisbon agenda. Prominent in these gatherings were Lord Peter Levene, chairman of Lloyd's of London, the insurance giant, and the former chief executive of Royal Dutch Shell, Jeroen van der Veer. These ruling class figures are not exactly military strategists, but their participation should reassure the international business community that their worldwide interests are being taken into consideration.

Indeed, a catalogue of threats enumerated by Rasmussen in a speech last year seemed to suggest that NATO was working for the insurance industry. NATO, he said, was needed to deal with piracy, cyber security, climate change, extreme weather events such as catastrophic storms and flooding, rising sea levels, large-scale population movement into inhabited areas, sometimes across borders, water shortages, droughts, decreasing food production, global warming, CO_2 emissions, the retreat of Arctic ice uncovering hitherto inaccessible resources, fuel efficiency and dependence on foreign sources, etc.

Most of the enumerated threats cannot even remotely be construed as calling for military solutions. Surely no 'rogue states' or 'outposts of tyranny' or 'international terrorists' are responsible for climate change, yet Rasmussen presents them as challenges to NATO. On the other hand, some of the results of these scenarios, such as population movements caused by rising sea levels or drought, can indeed be seen as potentially causing crises. The ominous aspect of the enumeration is precisely that all such problems are eagerly snatched up by NATO as requiring military solutions. The main threat to NATO is its own obsolescence. And the search for a 'strategic concept' is the search for pretexts to keep it going.

NATO's threat to the world

While it searches for threats, NATO itself is a growing threat to the world. The basic threat is its contribution to strengthening the US-led tendency to abandon diplomacy and negotiations in favour of military force. This is seen clearly in Rasmussen's inclusion of weather phenomena in his list of threats to NATO, when they should, instead, be problems for international diplomacy and negotiations. The growing danger is that Western diplomacy is dying. The United States has set the tone: we are virtuous, we have the power, the rest of the world must obey or else.

Diplomacy is despised as weakness. The State Department has long since ceased to be at the core of US foreign policy. With its vast network of military bases the world over, as well as military attachés in embassies and countless missions to client countries, the Pentagon is incomparably more powerful and influential in the world than the State Department.

Recent Secretaries of State, far from seeking diplomatic alternatives to war, have actually played a leading role in advocating war instead of diplomacy, whether Madeleine Albright in the Balkans or Colin Powell waving fake test tubes in the United Nations Security Council. Policy is defined by the National Security Advisor, various privately-funded think tanks, and the Pentagon, with interference from a Congress which itself is composed of politicians eager to obtain military contracts for their constituencies.

NATO is dragging Washington's European allies down the same path. Just as the Pentagon has replaced the State Department, NATO itself is being used by the United States as a potential substitute for the United Nations. The 1999 'Kosovo war' was a first major step in that direction. Sarkozy's France, after rejoining the NATO joint command, is gutting the traditionally skilled French foreign service, cutting back on civilian representation throughout the world. The European Union foreign service, now being created by Lady Ashton, will have no policy and no authority of its own.

Bureaucratic inertia

Behind its appeals to 'common values', NATO is driven, above all, by bureaucratic inertia. The alliance itself is an excrescence of the US military-industrial complex. For sixty years, military procurements and Pentagon contracts have been an essential source of industrial research, profits, jobs, Congressional careers, even university funding. The interplay of these varied interests converge to determine an implicit US strategy of world conquest:

- An ever-expanding global network of somewhere between 800 and a thousand military bases on foreign soil;
- Bilateral military accords with client states which offer training while obliging them to purchase US-made weapons and redesign their armed forces away from national defense toward internal security (i.e. repression) and possible integration into US-led wars of aggression;
- Use of these close relationships with local armed forces to influence the domestic politics of weaker states;
- Perpetual military exercises with client states, which provide the Pentagon with perfect knowledge of the military potential of client states, integrate them into the US military machine, and sustain a 'ready for war' mentality.
- Deployment of its network of bases, 'allies' and military exercises so as to surround, isolate, intimidate and eventually provoke major nations perceived as potential rivals, notably Russia and China.

The implicit strategy of the United States, as perceived by its actions, is a gradual military conquest to ensure world domination. One original feature of this world conquest project is that, although extremely active, day after day, it is virtually ignored by the vast majority of the population of the conquering nation, as well as by its most closely dominated allies, that is, the NATO states.

The endless propaganda about 'terrorist threats' (the fleas on the elephant) and other diversions keep most Americans totally unaware of what is going on, all the more easily in that Americans are almost uniquely ignorant of the rest of the world and, thus, totally uninterested. The US may bomb a country off the map before more than a small fraction of Americans know where to find it.

The main task of US strategists, whose careers take them between think tanks, boards of directors, consultancy firms and the government, is to justify this giant mechanism much more than to steer it. To a large extent, it steers itself.

Since the collapse of the 'Soviet threat', policy-makers have settled for invisible or potential threats. US military doctrine has as its aim to move preventively against any potential rival to US world hegemony. Since the collapse of the Soviet Union, Russia retains the largest arsenal outside the United States, and China is a rapidly rising economic power. Neither one threatens the United States or Western Europe. On the contrary, both are ready and willing to concentrate on peaceful business. However, they are increasingly alarmed by the military encirclement and provocative military exercises carried on by the United States on their very doorsteps. The implicit aggressive strategy may be obscure to most Americans, but leaders in the targeted countries are quite certain they understand what it is going on.

The Russia-Iran-Israel Triangle

Currently, the main explicit 'enemy' is Iran.

Washington claims that the 'missile shield' which it is forcing on its European allies is designed to defend the West from Iran. But the Russians see quite clearly that the missile shield is aimed at themselves. First of all, they understand quite clearly that Iran has no such missiles, nor any possible motive for using them against the West. It is perfectly obvious to all informed analysts that even if Iran developed nuclear weapons and missiles, they would be conceived as a deterrent against Israel, the regional nuclear superpower, which enjoys a free hand attacking neighboring countries. Israel does not want to lose that freedom to attack, and thus, naturally, opposes the Iranian deterrent.

Israeli propagandists scream loudly about the threat from Iran, and have worked incessantly to infect NATO with their paranoia. Israel has even been described as 'Global NATO's 29th member'. Israeli officials have assiduously worked on a receptive Madeleine Albright to make sure that Israeli interests are included in the 'Strategic Concept'. During the past five years, Israel and NATO have been taking part in joint naval exercises in the Red Sea and in the Mediterranean, as well as joint ground exercises from Brussels to Ukraine. On 16 October 2006, Israel became the first non-European country to reach a so-called 'Individual Co-operation Program' agreement with NATO for co-operation in 27 different areas. It is worth noting that Israel is the only country outside Europe which the US includes in the area of responsibility of its European Command (rather than the Central Command, which covers the rest of the Middle East).

At a NATO-Israel Relations seminar in Herzliya on 24 October 2006, the Israeli foreign minister at the time, Tzipi Livni, declared that 'The alliance between NATO and Israel is only natural ... Israel and NATO share a common strategic vision. In many ways, Israel is the front line defending our common way of life'.

Not everybody in European countries would consider that Israeli settlements in occupied Palestine reflect 'our common way of life'.

This is, no doubt, one reason why the deepening union between NATO and Israel has not taken the open form of NATO membership. Especially after the savage attack on Gaza, such a move would arouse objections in European countries. Nevertheless, Israel continues to invite itself into NATO, ardently supported, of course, by its faithful followers in the US Congress.

The principal cause of this growing Israel-NATO symbiosis has been identified by US writers John Mearsheimer and Stephen Walt: the vigorous and powerful pro-Israel lobby in the United States. Israeli lobbies are also strong in France and Britain. They have zealously developed the theme of Israel as the 'front line' in the defense of 'Western values' against militant Islam. The fact that militant Islam is largely a product of that 'front line' creates a perfect vicious circle. Israel's aggressive stance toward its regional neighbours would be a serious liability for NATO, apt to be dragged into wars of Israel's choosing which are by no means in the interest of Europe. However, there is one subtle strategic advantage in the Israeli connection which the United States seems to be using ... against Russia.

By subscribing to the hysterical 'Iranian threat' theory, the United States can continue to claim with a straight face that the planned missile shield is directed against Iran, not Russia. This cannot be expected to convince the Russians. But it can be used to make their protests sound 'paranoid' – at least to the ears of the Western faithful. Dear me, what can they be complaining about when we 'reset' our relations with Moscow and invite the Russian president to our 'Strategic Concept' happy gathering?

However, the Russians know quite well that:

● The missile shield is to be constructed surrounding Russia, which does have missiles, which it keeps for deterrence;

● By neutralizing Russian missiles, the United States would free its own hand to attack Russia, knowing that Russia could not retaliate.

Therefore, whatever is said, the missile shield, if it worked, would serve to facilitate eventual aggression against Russia.

Encircling Russia

The encirclement of Russia continues in the Black Sea, the Baltic and the Arctic Circle. United States officials continue to claim that Ukraine must join NATO. In a recent *New York Times* column, Zbigniew's son, Ian J. Brzezinski, advised Obama against abandoning the 'vision' of a 'whole, free and secure' Europe, including 'eventual Georgian and Ukrainian membership in NATO and the European Union'. The fact that the vast majority of the people of Ukraine are against NATO membership is of no account.

For the current scion of the noble Brzezinski dynasty it is the minority that counts. Abandoning the vision 'undercuts those in Georgia and Ukraine who see their future in Europe. It reinforces Kremlin aspirations for a sphere of influence … ' The notion that 'the Kremlin' aspires to a 'sphere of influence' in Ukraine is absurd considering the extremely close historic links between Russia and Ukraine, whose capital Kiev was the cradle of the Russian state. But the Brzezinski family hailed from Galicia, the part of Western Ukraine which once belonged to Poland, and which is the centre of the anti-Russian minority. US foreign policy is all too frequently influenced by such foreign rivalries, of which the vast majority of Americans are totally ignorant.

Relentless US insistence on absorbing Ukraine continues, despite the fact that it would imply expelling the Russian Black Sea fleet from its base in the Crimea peninsula, where the local population is overwhelmingly Russian-speaking and pro-Russian. This is a recipe for war with Russia if ever there was one.

And meanwhile, US officials continue to declare their support for Georgia, whose American-trained president openly hopes to bring NATO support into his next war against Russia.

Aside from provocative naval manoeuvres in the Black Sea, the United States, NATO, and (as yet) non-NATO members Sweden and Finland regularly carry out major military exercises in the Baltic Sea, virtually in sight of the Russian cities of Saint Petersburg and Kaliningrad. These exercises involve thousands of ground troops, hundreds of aircraft including F-15 jet fighters, AWACS, as well as naval forces, including the US Carrier Strike Group 12, landing craft and warships from a dozen countries.

Perhaps most ominous of all, in the Arctic region, the United States has been persistently engaging Canada and the Scandinavian states (including Denmark via Greenland) in a military deployment openly directed against Russia. The point of these Arctic deployments was stated by Fogh Rasmussen when he mentioned, among 'threats' to be met by NATO, the fact that 'Arctic ice is retreating, for resources that had, until now, been covered under ice'.

Now, one might consider that this uncovering of resources would be an opportunity for cooperation in exploiting them. But that is not the official US mindset. Last October, US Admiral James G Stavridis, supreme Nato commander for Europe, said global warming and a race for resources could lead to a conflict in the Arctic. Coast Guard Rear Admiral Christopher C. Colvin, in charge of Alaska's coastline, said Russian shipping activity in the Arctic Ocean was 'of particular concern' for the US, and called for more military facilities in the region.

The US Geological Service believes that the Arctic contains up to a quarter of the world's unexplored deposits of oil and gas. Under the 1982 United Nations Law of the Sea Convention, a coastal state is entitled to a 200-nautical mile exclusive economic zone, and can claim a further 150 miles if it proves that the seabed is a continuation of its continental shelf. Russia is applying to make this claim.

After pushing for the rest of the world to adopt the Convention, the United States Senate has still not ratified the Treaty.

In January 2009, NATO declared the 'High North' to be 'of strategic interest to the Alliance', and since then, NATO has held several major war games clearly preparing for eventual conflict with Russia over Arctic resources. Russia largely dismantled its defenses in the Arctic after the collapse of the Soviet Union, and has called for negotiating compromises over resource control.

Last September, Prime Minister Vladimir Putin called for joint efforts to protect the fragile ecosystem, attract foreign investment, promote environmentally friendly technologies, and work to resolve disputes through international law. But the United States, as usual, prefers to settle the issue by throwing its weight around. This could lead to a new arms race in the Arctic, and even to armed clashes.

Despite all these provocative moves, it is most unlikely that the United States actually seeks war with Russia, although skirmishes and incidents here and there cannot be ruled out. The US policy appears to be to encircle and intimidate Russia to such an extent that it accepts a semi-satellite status which neutralizes it in the anticipated future conflict with China.

Target China

The only reason to target China is like the proverbial reason to climb the mountain: it is there. It is big. And the US must be on top of everything.

The strategy for dominating China is the same as for Russia. It is classic warfare: encirclement, siege, more or less clandestine support for internal disorder. As examples of this strategy:

● The United States is provocatively strengthening its military presence along the Pacific shores of China, offering 'protection against China' to East Asian countries.

● During the Cold War, when India got its armaments from the Soviet Union and struck a non-aligned posture, the United States armed Pakistan as its main regional ally. Now the US is shifting its favours to India, in order to keep India out of the orbit of the Shanghai Co-operation Organization and to build it as a counterweight to China.

● The United States and its allies support any internal dissidence that might weaken China, whether it is the Dalai Lama, the Uighurs, or Liu Xiaobo, the jailed dissident.

The Nobel Peace Prize was bestowed on Liu Xiaobo by a committee of Norwegian legislators headed by Thorbjorn Jagland, Norway's echo of Tony Blair, who has served as Norway's prime minister and foreign minister, and has been one of his country's main cheerleaders for NATO. At a NATO-sponsored conference of European parliamentarians last year, Jagland declared: 'when we are not able to stop tyranny, war starts. This is why NATO is indispensable. NATO is the only multilateral military organization rooted in international law. It is an organization that the UN can use when necessary – to stop tyranny, like we did in the Balkans.' This is an astoundingly bold mis-statement of fact, considering that NATO openly defied international law and the United Nations to make war in the Balkans – where, in reality, there was ethnic conflict, but no 'tyranny'.

In announcing the choice of Liu, the Norwegian Nobel committee, headed by Jagland, declared that it 'has long believed that there is a close connection between human rights and peace'. The 'close connection', to follow the logic of Jagland's own statements, is that if a foreign state fails to respect human rights according to Western interpretations, it may be bombed, as NATO bombed Yugoslavia. Indeed, the very powers that make the most noise about 'human rights', notably the United States and Britain, are the ones making the most wars all over the world. The Norwegian's statements make it clear that granting the Nobel Peace Prize to Liu (who in his youth spent time in Norway) amounted, in reality, to an endorsement of NATO.

'Democracies' to replace the United Nations

The European members of NATO add relatively little to the military power of the United States. Their contribution is above all political. Their presence maintains the illusion of an 'International Community'. The world conquest being pursued by the bureaucratic inertia of the Pentagon can be presented as the crusade by the world's 'democracies' to spread their enlightened political order to the rest of a recalcitrant world.

The Euro-Atlantic governments proclaim their 'democracy' as proof of their absolute right to intervene in the affairs of the rest of the world. On the basis of the fallacy that 'human rights are necessary for peace', they proclaim their right to make war. A crucial question is whether 'Western democracy' still has the strength to dismantle this war machine before it is too late.

Author's note: Grateful thanks to Rick Rozoff for his constant flow of important information (contact b-antinato@yahoogroups.com).

Published with grateful acknowledgements to Global Research (www.globalresearch.ca).

Regime change or disarming WMD?

Blair's contradictions

Lynne Jones

Lynne Jones was, until April 2010, the distinguished Member of Parliament for Birmingham Selly Oak. This excerpt is from her detailed submission to the Iraq Inquiry under Sir John Chilcot, prepared with the assistance of Ingrid Davidson. The Inquiry had sought the views of MPs, but then declined to publish them. The full submission is available online.

Legally, regime change and disarmament of Iraqi WMD via the United Nations were two separate and different bases for war. We know that it would not have been possible to get a legal agreement for war on the basis of regime change and this was made clear to Tony Blair in a letter from Jack Straw dated 25 March 2002. Tony Blair was told this again in July 2002 in the 'Downing Street Memo'. This records that the Attorney-General told the Prime Minister that the desire for regime change was not a legal base for military action. Yet, in his evidence to your inquiry, Tony Blair tries to 'merge' the two distinct rationales for going to war:

> 'I think there is a danger that we end up with a very sort of binary distinction between regime change here and WMD here.'

He continued with this point as he was questioned further:

> 'It is more a different way of expressing the same proposition. The Americans in a sense were saying, "We are for regime change because we don't trust he is ever going to give up his WMD ambitions". We were saying, "We have to deal with his WMD ambitions. If that means regime change, so be it".'

I urge the Inquiry panel to consider this very closely. Saying 'we are going to remove a regime from power because we think it poses a threat' is not the same as saying 'we want to make a regime complaint with international obligations on WMD and will use force to achieve this if necessary'. Whilst the outcome of these two rationales for using force could be the same (regime change) the objectives are clearly distinct.

A number of statements by Tony Blair in the run up to the war show that in seeking support for his policy towards Iraq, he repeatedly made use of the clear distinction between the policies of regime change and disarmament. On the day the Government's September 2002 dossier was launched in the House of Commons, Tony Blair was asked if regime change was his objective and he replied that it was not:

'Regime change in Iraq would be a wonderful thing. That is not the purpose of our action; our purpose is to disarm Iraq of weapons of mass destruction ...'

He made the distinction between regime change and disarmament again, on 25 February 2003:

'I detest his [Saddam Hussein's] regime – I hope most people do – but even now, he could save it by complying with the UN's demand. Even now, we are prepared to go the extra step to achieve disarmament peacefully.'

And, on 18 March 2003, in his speech in favour of the resolution for war, Tony Blair told MPs that regime change was never the justification for military action:

'I have never put the justification for action as regime change. We have to act within the terms set out in resolution 1441 – that is our legal base.'

Tony Blair made a clear distinction between the two policies for political reasons as well as legal reasons. The public UK policy that Iraq had to disarm left open the possibility for Saddam Hussein to comply with the demands made on him, via UN resolutions, and for his regime to continue. This argument was used by Tony Blair to suggest that UK policy was in line with the principle that it should be left to the people of individual nations to change their regime/government, unless pre-emptive military action is needed either to avert an overwhelming humanitarian catastrophe or for self defence and that there must be international consensus that this is the case (i.e. through the UN).

The principle is there because of the innumerable ramifications for the long-term future of a country, its region and world stability when one government is overthrown by another. The distinction between US-led regime change on the one hand, and international action with UN authorisation on the other, was very live within the Parliamentary Labour Party (PLP) in 2002/2003. Without majority PLP support, Parliamentary authority for the use of force might not have been won. The case that Tony Blair put to doubting colleagues was that regime change was not the basis for UK involvement and that he personally considered Saddam Hussein to be both a current and long-term threat because of WMD.

Regime change by outside military force and the disarmament of Iraq's weapons of mass destruction capability via the UN were two distinct and separate policy objectives, both politically and legally. Tony Blair clearly told the House that regime change was not the purpose of military action in Iraq. The question is, was he misleading the House?

* * *

Did Tony Blair commit the United Kingdom to the policy of regime change?

Your Inquiry questioned Tony Blair about whether he signed the UK up to military action during his private meeting with George Bush at his Crawford ranch in April 2002. He responded that the essence of his assurance to George Bush was only that 'we are going to be with you in confronting and dealing with this threat' and that his private position was no different from his public position. Tony Blair sites the evidence of his Prime Ministerial foreign policy adviser, Sir David Manning, to back up the assertion that he had not committed the UK to a policy of regime change. In his evidence to you, David Manning appears to confirm this:

> 'Our view, the Prime Minsiter's view, the British Government's view throughout this episode was that the aim was disarmament. It was not regime change.'

However, a leaked memo from Sir David Manning to the Prime Minister dated 14 March 2002, reporting on discussions in Washington with US Secretary of State, Condoleezza Rice, clearly records that Tony Blair had committed the UK to a policy of regime change and that Sir David Manning was fully aware of this and the ramifications for managing this position in public:

> 'I said [to Condoleezza Rice] that you would not budge in your support for regime change but you had to manage a press, a parliament and a public opinion that was very different than anything in the States.'

After writing this memo, Sir David Manning remained the Prime Minister's Foreign Policy adviser and was subsequently promoted to be British Ambassador to Washington. It is therefore fair to presume that David Manning accurately transmitted Tony Blair's view to the US administration.

The Chilcot Inquiry was criticised in the press for not raising the 14 March 2002 memo from Sir David Manning to the Prime Minister with Sir

David. I urge the Panel to take this memo into consideration if it has not been made available to them from source and to comment on the discrepancy between this memo and the evidence given by Tony Blair and Sir David that the British Government's objective was not regime change.

Evidence from the UK's Ambassador to Washington, Sir Christopher Meyer, is also that Tony Blair had committed to regime change by March 2002, and he makes reference to a memo he sent to Sir David Manning on 18 March 2002 in which he stated:

> 'I opened by sticking very closely to the script that you used with Condi Rice. We backed regime change, but the plan had to be clever and failure was not an option. It would be a tough sell for us domestically, and probably tougher elsewhere in Europe.'

The memos referred to above are the closest to any high level record of UK policy on Iraq in early to mid 2002. They lend considerable weight to the conclusion that Tony Blair did commit to a policy of regime change, but knowing this would be difficult to 'sell', went about trying to secure international and domestic support for military action on the basis of the different stated objective of compliance with UN resolutions on disarmament.

Tony Blair's assertion that he did not sign up for regime change in March/April 2002 thus has little credibility and neither has his later argument that the policies of regime change and disarmament with respect to Iraq in 2002/2003 were 'a different way of expressing the same proposition'.

www.lynnejones.org.uk

Blair's Blunder

'I would still have thought it right to remove him. I mean obviously you would have had to use and deploy different arguments, about the nature of the threat ... I can't really think we'd be better with him and his two sons still in charge ...'

Tony Blair's reply to Fern Britton about Saddam Hussein, broadcast on BBC television in December 2009, when she asked whether he would still have gone on with plans to join the US-led invasion of Iraq had he known at the time that there were no weapons of mass destruction in the country.

Basil Davidson

A memory

Michael Barratt Brown

Basil Davidson died in July 2010. Michael Barratt Brown, his lifelong friend, spoke at his funeral. We follow Michael's words with a small sample of Basil's own work; his review of a book about the Second World War. We hope this might, in some small way, introduce new readers to Basil Davidson's outstanding work over a long and eventful life.

It would be impossible for me ever to forget the impression that Basil made on me on one of the first occasions that I met him some 60 years ago. He had just come out of Yugoslavia where he had been parachuted into largely enemy held territory as a British liaison officer with Partisan forces in the Vojvodina. It was in a villa just outside Bari, where I was leading a small advance unit of a Yugoslav mission of the United Nations Relief and Rehabilitation Administration (UNRRA) stationed there, preparing to enter Yugoslavia as the German armies withdrew under intense Partisan pressure. I had asked Basil to come to speak to us about what we might expect when we met up with the civil authorities which the Partisans were establishing in territory which they had liberated. He was a toweringly impressive, rather austere, figure, very tall and slim, clothed in a rather splendid battle dress made of some green waterproof material, with a rather fetching cravat at the top and enormous boots at the bottom.

But what he had to tell us was riveting. Some of us from Britain had already met some of Tito's Partisans in refugee camps in Egypt where we had been working, and had got some understanding of the extraordinary capacity for democratic organisation that they were capable of. Our attitude was in strong contrast to that of other Brits who had an army background and had imbibed strong colonial attitudes. Others still coming straight from the United States were deeply suspicious of anything smelling of Communism. Basil won us all over, not by any romantic picture of guerrilla armies and heroic deeds against fearful odds, though we could imagine these. What he gave us was a very simple down to earth description of peasant families organising themselves quietly and efficiently to defend themselves and their villages from a brutal occupation, involving the collaboration of many of their own people. Basil explained to us something of the structure of local and district and county committees held together by a multi-ethnic Assembly and government, which had already been meeting in liberated territory. Basil described something of this experience in his book *Special Operations Europe,* published by Gollancz in 1980, which I most strongly recommend as a complement to his African studies.

Some of this Partisan experience of Basil's we in UNRRA already knew from the reports which we had received from the British Military Mission of which Basil was a member. But what Basil added to the story, as a trained journalist as well as a seasoned soldier, was the simple humanity of the men and women involved, drawn as they were from several ethnic groups, which the Germans were anxious to divide in order to conquer, but which Tito's Partisans were seeking in every way to unite against a common enemy. When I got into Yugoslavia and drove inland over the mountains to reach Sarajevo, just a few days after the Germans had left, I found that what Basil had told us was true. I had to talk to local committees about getting food supplies in from outside. I found that these committees always included representatives from each of the local ethnic groups, all determined to work together to rebuild their country after the terrible destruction that the occupiers had wrought.

I still believe in the capacity of the Yugoslav peoples to work together – and have written about this – in spite of the civil wars of the 1990s, which once again, as so often before in Yugoslav history, were incited and inflamed by outside forces with their own several ambitions – Turks, Austrians, Hungarians, Italians, Germans, and now Americans. What Basil learnt from those brave Partisans gave him the courage and the understanding for his subsequent defence of the liberation struggles of the African peoples and his continuing faith that, one day, they will win. What I could hardly have guessed from those early meetings 60 years ago was that they would lead to a lifetime's close personal friendship with Basil and Marion.

*   *   *

What really happened?

In 1996, at Ken Coates' suggestion, Basil Davidson wrote this review of a substantial new history* of the Second World War. It was originally published in European Labour Forum *journal (no.17).*

What the Second World War meant to all of us in Europe is a vast and painful subject which eventually, maybe in 50 years of so, will be summarised in a balanced and 'definitive' judgment. Meanwhile, as the old millennium draws to its close, there is now a good place for summaries which tell us, in a reasonably comprehensive and reliable way, what actually happened after Hitler's armies marched into Poland in September 1939 and the killing and burning seriously began. How was the war fought through those terrible years? Who did the bulk of the fighting, and with what overall objectives in view? Weinberg is an American historian who attempts some answers which will hold good for the present and immediate future. In a huge book scaled to the massive size of his under-taking, he gives us what appears to me – a serving soldier through that war but by no means a military historian – a remarkably successful response to such questions. Free in his judgements of the main *dramatis personae*, he is bound to run into serious dissent here and there, notably in relation to some aspects of the archival sources – but generally he encourages a sense of confidence in what he has to tell and in his manner of telling it.

His book moves with impressive ease and competence from the initial nazi aggressions of 1939 and early 1940 to the enormous campaigns of killing and destruction in which Hitler developed his aims of world-wide conquest. Here Weinberg remains true to his initial organising principle: as in his earlier books on the background to the war, to his well-nourished conviction that 'the course of German foreign policy provides the obvious organising principle for any account of the origins of World War Two'. In short, the aims and objectives and methods of the Nazi Party, and centrally of Hitler himself, were and remained at least until 1943, by which time the tide had begun to turn, the central dynamic of all this horrific warfare and destruction. With a powerful command of his military material, Weinberg has composed a genuine *tour de force*.

How did Hitler's plans unfold after his destruction of the French army in 1940 and his somewhat later invasion of the Soviet Union? While the Western Allies, essentially Britain alone until late in 1941, strove to meet their expulsion from the European mainland by the then called *Festung Europa,* what happened on the vast 'Eastern Front'? Weinberg usefully expounds the course of all that in a lucid account of the *Wehrmacht's* engulfment of the Low Countries and the Scandinavian states while its legions pressed home their assault as far as the very crests of the Caucasus, the approaches to the Nile Valley, and on all the lands between. Weinberg does all this with skill, and everything that critically mattered seems to be somewhere here: the titanic struggle across the oceans, the unbending and always malicious violence of Hitler's planning and commitment, whether on the war fronts or in the civilian rear, the endless massacres wherever the *Wehrmacht* could reach, and the various and bestial designs and 'measures' by which Hitler's Europe was to be rendered worthy of the Aryan master race. Weinberg goes on to recount the war in Asia, and again does so in a way that usefully shows how Japanese imperialism, in its turn, was duly overcome and humbled in the dust.

There are, of course, some oddities of Weinbergian judgement; and no doubt on this wide canvas it could scarcely have been otherwise. Weinberg's view of the famous confrontation between Hitler and Chamberlain, at Munich in 1938, is that the 'Munich Agreement' was a stiff defeat for Hitler and his plans. European judgement, then and since, has been exactly the reverse. By delivering the Czechoslovak Republic and its powerful army into Nazi hands, Chamberlain's 'peace in our time' (as Chamberlain claimed) ensured the subjection of the Poles and laid open the way to the defeat of France and invasion of the USSR. Weinberg quotes his previous books in support of what can only seem a perverse judgement on the realities that followed 'Munich', but these I have not read.

Some other aspects will give the admiring reader pause, a very insufficient handling of the campaign in Italy being one of them. But generally Weinberg's method suffers most, even if understandably for a writer clearly given to a complete self-confidence, from a wish to suggest omniscience. He has read widely in the available archives, yet he has not always read enough. On minor points he is thus rather easily led astray. In the matter of the British decision to shift military support from the monarchist 'chetniks' in Serbia to the Communist-led partisans he is content to recite some very foolish gossip by monarchist writers in the USA, although the hard-and-fast reasons for that well-known 'switch' of British military effort are perfectly clear in the archives and their official commentaries. His severe criticisms of some of the British deception ploys in the lead-up to the Normandy landings of 1944 are sharply at odds, again, with British official histories based on archives still not completely available to the public. On all major issues, however, he is surely well based. Which is why his work will be welcomed as a useful reminder of what the military history of World War Two was really about.

A World at Arms: A Global History of World War Two, Gerhard L. Weinberg, Cambridge University Press, 1178pp.

Reviews

On the River Thames

Harry Gosling, *Up and Down Stream*, with a new foreword by Ken Coates, published by Spokesman as a Trade Union Classic, with 20 illustrations, 300 pages including 20 illustrations, paperback ISBN 9780851247786, £19.95

It is to the great credit of Spokesman publishers that they have brought out a new edition of this outstanding book, first published in 1927. It is an autobiography of a trade union leader who was born in very humble circumstances nearly 150 years ago. But it is much more than an autobiography. It provides a gripping account of the trade union organisation of transport workers, particularly dockworkers, and draws lessons from every phase of the struggle. These lessons are still relevant today. *Up and Down Stream* is, indeed, much more than a compellingly interesting story of a man's life. It is in many ways a textbook for effective trade union organisation. My interest when reading it never faltered from the first page to the last.

Harry Gosling was born in 1861 in North Lambeth, very near to the south bank of the River Thames. His family life was bound up with work on the river. He could trace this connection back to his great grandfather, who was a bargeman, apprenticed in the 1780s. Harry continued the family tradition and became an apprentice when he was 14 years of age. He soon learnt that he had joined a group of workers who, conscious of their skill and mutual dependence on each other, had a strong sense of solidarity. Their work demanded both physical strength and skill. They depended upon each other for safety. His own words speak volumes:

'One of their most pronounced traits is perhaps their inherent trust in each other ... The absolute dependence of one man on another creates a bond between them which is almost as strong as a blood tie ... The endless variety of circumstances, the change of wind and weather, the calls upon each other for help produce this ...'

Gosling conveys vividly the need for skill and care in navigating a busy river in a barge, sometimes towing logs, avoiding obstacles in a busy port, navigating passage under bridges, avoiding other craft, and checking and dealing constantly with changes in the weather, wind and tide.

In 1887, Harry Gosling fell ill and he was away from work on the river for a period of about three years. He thus missed the historic dock strike of 1889. Nevertheless, he maintained his interest in his occupation and during his recovery he was asked to do some work for the Amalgamated Society of Watermen and Lightermen of the River Thames, which he had earlier joined. In 1890 he was elected president of the Lambeth branch and representative on the Executive Council. Early in 1893, he was elected as General Secretary of the union. In the same year he also attended the TUC for the first time as a delegate from his union. He recalls that the Congress had a 'full dress' debate on socialism and a resolution was carried in favour of independent labour representation.

During his period as General Secretary of his union, Harry Gosling played a leading role in securing improved working conditions on the river. As a result of the1889 dock strike the working day for men and boys was reduced to 12, to be worked at any time between 6am and 8pm. Some of the companies sought to interpret the agreement to warrant a working day spread over 14 hours. This eventually led to a 17-week strike among the men in 1900 and a further strike in 1909. The apprentices' strike led to the appointment of an arbitrator by the Board of Trade. The apprentices' claim was upheld.

Harry Gosling was also politically active. He served on the London County Council for 27 years. His first attempt to secure election was in 1895, when he fought the riverside seat of Rotherhithe as a Labour-Progressive candidate, years before the formation of the Labour Party. He was unsuccessful. Three years later he was again unsuccessful when he stood for Clapham. Soon after, however, he was nominated for an aldermanic seat on the Council and, with the support of the small Labour group and the Progressives, he was elected.

In 1904, Harry Gosling was elected to the LCC for the East End constituency of St. George's and Wapping. It was a constituency which, in his own words, 'abounded in stories of hunger – hunger and hopelessness together'. Nevertheless he spoke well of the unselfishness of many of his constituents.

Harry Gosling was an LCC member at the time of the famous dispute affecting Poplar councillors. Because of its poverty and unemployment, Poplar had a very high level of rates. The residents were, in effect, paying to relieve their own poverty. Poplar was also required, as every other London borough, to pay precepts to the London County Council, the Metropolitan Police and the Metropolitan Asylum Board. Poplar's Labour councillors called for the equalisation of rates over the whole of London to meet all local services. To draw attention to the injustice under which they were forced to levy extremely high rates on their own citizens, they decided not to levy rates to cover the central precepts.

The rebel councillors were ultimately sent to prison for contempt of court. Harry Gosling took a leading role in the campaign to secure their release. One of his collaborators was a young, able and energetic lawyer, W. H. Thompson (founder of the well-known law firm which, over many years right up to the present time, has rendered great service to the unions and to millions of working people). In the end a formula was found to secure the release of the imprisoned councillors.

One of the chapters in Harry Gosling's book is devoted to the establishment of the Port of London Authority. It was the subject of sharp political division. As far back as the year 1900 a Royal Commission had pointed out that the Port was in danger of losing part of its trade because of the inadequacies of its channels and docks. The numerous companies with interests in London shipping were unable to cope with the gigantic problem. In the words of Harry Gosling:

> 'In short, unification of control was an absolute necessity in order to end this disastrous state of affairs, and the Port of London Authority was created to save a vital national concern that capitalism and conflicting private interests had all but ruined.'

The PLA eventually came into existence in 1909. Lloyd George was influential in securing the much-needed reform.

Harry Gosling describes at length the struggle to achieve trade union federation among dockworkers and within the wider transport industries. It was not easy, particularly among groups with a strong craft identity. At times he even became impatient with some of his own members. It was Tom Mann, he recalls, who urged him, 'to stay where you are and bring them along with you'.

Gosling gives Ben Tillett, at that time the General Secretary of the Dockers' Union, the main credit for the formation of the National Transport Workers' Federation, in 1910-11. Gosling was elected President of the new Federation. It did good work, but was soon involved in a national dispute which led to a strike of more than 100,000 men. An agreement was finally secured which brought concessions to every section of port workers.

This, however, was not the end of the story. Some of the old problems remained unresolved and, in May 1912, the dispute re-opened. It led to a national strike, but the employers were determined not to make concessions. The men, according to Gosling, were eventually defeated by sheer starvation.

Gosling's view was that the unions failed in 1912 because a trade union federation, representing nearly thirty unions, each with its own executive council, was not always a suitable body to promote trade union solidarity in a national strike. His view on this weakness was strengthened by the failure known as 'Black Friday', in 1921, when the Triple Alliance of miners, railwaymen and transport workers was no more than 'a glorified federation and as such it failed'. In 1921, Harry Gosling was the vice-chairman of the Triple Alliance and witnessed at first hand the defeat of the unions.

Harry Gosling was thus a firm advocate of trade union amalgamation. He was in no doubt that Ernest Bevin was mainly responsible for the success of establishing the Transport and General Workers' Union. He speaks of 'his extraordinary vigour and perseverance', and points out that considerable impetus was given to the transports workers' amalgamation by Bevin's advocacy before the Dockers' Court of Enquiry under Lord Shaw in 1921.

Lord Shaw produced a condemnatory report of conditions on the docks. He said that, 'the system of casualisation must, if possible, be torn up by the roots'. It was one of the most forthright reports ever published on labour conditions.

Harry Gosling became founding President of the T&GWU. It was a worthy tribute to his contribution to trade union unity. In 1923, he was elected to Parliament as a member for Whitechapel in the East End of London. In the following year, with the election of the first minority Labour Government, he was appointed Minister of Transport.

Throughout his trade union life Harry Gosling was a strong advocate of international solidarity and international institutions to promote social progress. He always spoke warmly, for example, of the work of the Independent Labour Organisation in seeking to promote better working conditions throughout the world, including collective bargaining, a short working week, the abolition of child labour, equal pay for work of equal value, and safe working conditions.

Harry Gosling's humanity was shown, also, in his wide range of interests. He helped to promote the Workers' Travel Association, he served on the Civil Service Arbitration Board, and was a member of the War Graves Commission. He spoke warmly of the decision that all graves, whatever the rank of the dead service-person, should be marked alike.

Harry Gosling died in 1930. He was still an MP. He deserves to be remembered as a good man, a fine trade unionist and a great credit to the class into which he was born and whose interests he so well represented.

I enjoyed this book immensely.

J. E. Mortimer

Power and ideology

Justin Fox, *The Myth of the Rational Market: A History of Risk, Reward, and Delusion on Wall Street,* **Harriman House, 2009, 382 pages, hardback ISBN 9781906659691, £18.99.**
Jérôme Gautié and John Schmitt, editors, *Low-Wage Work in the Wealthy World,* **Russell Sage Foundation, New York, 2010, 486 pages, hardback ISBN 9780871540614, $45**
Mary Mellor, *The Future of Money; From Financial Crisis to Public Resource,* **Pluto Press, 2010, 198 pages, paperback ISBN 9780745329949, £17.99**

What a sorry state we are in. From low wages to financial speculation, backed up by theoretical nonsense about how rational it all is supposed to be. These books, in their different ways, demonstrate the power of ideology behind the alleged 'science' of economics. They are powerful contributions to an understanding of the structure of economies, the structure of income, and the role of money – money itself being not just an abstract denominator of exchange value but also a political instrument.

Part of the ideology is the myth of 'not bucking the market'. One could add that, if the market produces what is described in these three books, we should think again. But it is not so straightforward. Let us consider this in more detail.

(1) *Money, and the power of debt; or, philosophy and economics*
Mellor alleges that the state surrendered its role of creating money to the private sector – borrowing and indebtedness. I am not so sure that this is such a recent event since the old merchant banking families, such as the Italian Lombards, and then the Rothschilds, made their money, either raising it for governments fighting European or civil wars (Lombards), or speculating on gilts (Rothschild) in the event of Napoleonic defeat. This was the private sector at its free-market best. But what did it all produce, or endorse? War, one supposes. So the markets in debt and securities were based on financing conflict, as I suggest is the situation currently. Nothing has really changed for a thousand years. It's not 'capitalism', but the use of finance for aggressive means.

At the same time as I was reading these books, I started to read Michael Mansfield's autobiography, *Memoirs of a Radical Lawyer*. It hit the nail on the head. He comments on the miners' strike and its aftermath (he defended the strikers at Orgreave Colliery who faced apparent trumped-up charges). His descriptions echoed the themes of these three books.

> 'But the much-acclaimed victory of capital, and the demise of union power, has been a hollow and short-lived affair. It heralded unmitigated privatisation, untrammelled deregulation, and the growth of a society built on asset-stripping, self-interest and a culture of unabashed bonanza bonuses.' (p.84)

This from a respected QC.

(2) *Theoretical underpinnings*

The analysis is about the role and definition of 'market'. This is a fascinating concept to explore.

Mellor's book is slightly tedious and misses the point. I wrote in the margin at one point that it was a glorified book review, but there are some insights. Many of the facts and references are well known. She explains perfectly the diminished role of the state versus the private sector in finance. But is it diminished? One could argue that the role of the state is, or has had to be, more prominent than ever – bailing out the collapsed rational market theory which underpins modern definitions of risk and reward. Fox reminds us, in a social-anthropological fashion, detailing who was who in the construction of an economic theory which became ascendant in governments and academia during the rise of financial market dominance, that it was almost religious. It was based on *a priori* assumptions about the random decisions of countless others always proving right if only the state would get out of the way: the rule of the market. In this reviewer's opinion, the 'market' as a concept is political.

For example, as Mellor pleads,

> 'Money is too important to be left to the market.' (p.30)

I was not sure what this meant, unless one looks at power structures.

The books, jointly, explain the chaos, although there are no surprises.

(3) *Consequences for people*

The role of class in the analysis of the market

What emerges is that the so-called market is not a random collection of rational people maximising their utility, but a structure of exploitation. This may sound obvious to readers, but the books prove it, yet again. The Chicago School, led by Milton Friedman, whose lectures attracted audiences like a rock star, explained in Fox's exposition of personalities in this economic cock-up, went on to screw up Chile, that is, privatise pensions (with plaudits from the World Bank, endorsed by US Secretary of

State), introduce massive discrimination against women, while condoning the killing of 9,000 citizens, although this crime against humanity is not mentioned in any of the books.

The rational market was dependent on military rule and violence against radicals and trade unions. The market, if it exists as its advocates would like, is basically inhuman. This is the inference from the books.

The low-wage report considers, in particular, Denmark, Germany, France, The Netherlands, the United Kingdom and the United States. There are some surprising results, which appear to demonstrate the power of labour in confronting market 'rationality', despite declining union membership in all of these countries. Denmark apparently shows how the market and social partners can work together. But the table on page 106 reveals that there is no National Minimum Wage but a national wage floor – which some firms do not implement. In Germany 'an increasing number of firms are withdrawing from industry collective agreements'.

Mellor goes on to explain the all-important role of debt. The low wage book explains, by implication, who pays for it, the rational market book outlines how we delude ourselves about the motives of the key actors. My commentary is that the ideology, or hegemony, of finance has distributional consequences. What some call 'financialisation', like a cultural phenomenon or disease, is nothing of the sort. It is about a power structure, backed up by an ideology, a creed.

Mellor states that money/finance is based on trust, and the market cannot provide it.

> 'Money circulation through the financial system is seen as the outcome of private economic acts, not as a function of social relationships and public authority.' (p. 2)

To conclude, we should examine very carefully the use of concepts such as 'market', 'rationality', 'risk', 'finance', 'wage' and 'class'. Most of all we should look at the actual structure of finance and the labour relations behind it all. The use of language is important, and disguises power relations and distributional issues.

There is more to be written.

Richard Minns

Reference

Michael Mansfield, *Memoirs of a Radical Lawyer,* (with Yvette Vanson), Bloomsbury, 2009

Attlee

Attlee's Great Contemporaries, **edited by Frank Field, Continuum, 240 pages, hardback ISBN 9780826432247, £17.99**

This is a delightful collection of articles, published between 1951 and 1966, mainly in *The Observer*, and written in the style of Attlee the statesman, 'terse, telling and to the point', as Peter Hennessy puts it in the epilogue. There are three threads running through them: Attlee's relationships with Churchill, the United States, and the Labour Party. One should not be fooled by the austere image of Attlee. It is just that, an image, no less than the self-propagated, more flamboyant image of Churchill.

Today, we are well aware that a politician's character and public image can be far apart; a growing gap which has contributed to the public distrust of the whole political class. The editor, Frank Field, suggests that in politics character is all, and asks us to compare the characters of Attlee and Churchill. The book's title echoes one of Churchill's own books, *Great Contemporaries* (implying in Churchill's case, presumably, that I am great and these are my contemporaries.)

The subtitle is 'the politics of character'. Field's thesis, expressed in an introductory essay, is that the key to successful political leadership is character. He quotes Attlee approvingly:

> 'there are many men who find it impossible to believe that men lead other men other than by example of moral and physical courage: sympathy, self-discipline, altruism, and superior capacity for hard work.'

Field argues that Attlee drew his sense of 'duty, loyalty and responsibility' from being bought up in the Anglican Church and his belief in Christian ethics. Yet, as Kenneth Harris points out in his biography of Attlee, one thing Attlee learned at Haileybury was that he did not believe in God: 'So far as I was concerned it was mumbo-jumbo'.[1]

So where do Attlee's ethics come from? Kenneth Morgan charts Attlee's intellectual conversion from a young conservative into a socialist, via Carlyle's study of *Chartism*, Ruskin's *Unto this Last*, and the writings of William Morris. Indeed, Attlee's favourite passage came from *A Dream of John Ball*,

> 'Forsooth, brothers. Fellowship is heaven and lack of fellowship is hell, fellowship is life and lack of fellowship is death: and the deeds you do upon this earth it is for fellowship's sake ye do them.'

Attlee was a great lover of literature and poetry. One of the most telling pieces, which gives a great insight into Attlee's 'character', is *The Pleasure of Books*. Here he describes his library and how much his books are like a collection of old friends, and what they mean to him. He was of the generation that not only enjoyed Morris's prose but also his poetry, which many of us, today, find hard going. He had few rare books or first editions; for him books were for reading, not collecting. But he did have three books by Morris from the Kelmscott Press, 'the gift of some kind friends in the socialist movement, who knew where my love abided'.

One of the reasons Attlee wrote these pieces was because he needed the money to house his library. He had given up his own home in 1945, on moving into Downing Street, because of the housing shortage. Yet, sensing his political mortality, and looking forward to only a modest pension, as Field puts it, he and Vi sought a new home. 'Whatever else this house needed, a primary purpose for Attlee was to house his books.'

Attlee was a complex personality who rose to be Prime Minister, yet, in his early political life, he could not get elected to Stepney Borough Council. He had done the hard yards as a street corner orator, discovering in the process the people he most admired: 'those who did the tedious jobs, collecting our exiguous subscriptions, trying to sell literature, and carrying the impoverished platform from one street corner to another. They got no glamour. They did not expect to see victory, but uncomplainingly, they worked to try and help the cause.'[2] Maybe he sounds so passionate about the foot soldiers in the movement, having been one of them himself.

Attlee called himself a socialist, but of what kind? His 'socialism' was, as he points out in his autobiography when writing about the Independent Labour Party, 'a way of life rather than an economic dogma'. He believed, like Keir Hardie, that a party based on the simple object of getting Labour representatives into Parliament was 'bound in time to become socialist'.[3]

The most telling contributions to this collection, which includes a wide range of pieces, are those on Churchill and the wartime generals, which reveal Attlee's view of the United States, and those on Labour figures. The relationship with Churchill is a major theme, and Attlee certainly has the measure of him: 'He was always looking around for "finest hours" and if one was not immediately available, his impulse was to manufacture one.' (p.161)

In his reviews of the memoirs of Generals Allenbroke, Montgomery and Marshall he lets us know his views of the United States. He feels they were so obsessed with the British Empire they missed out on the growing Russian one: 'The Americans were indeed innocents abroad. It is ironical to reflect when one considers their present attitude to the Communist peril, how much they contributed to its extension westward'.

There are excellent portraits of Hardie, Lansbury and Bevan, but the most telling one is of Ernest Bevin. They were a formidable team. Bevin was for Attlee the embodiment of a 'Labour representative in parliament'. In 'A Man of Power', in this collection, Attlee points out that,

> 'The main thing that Bevin did for the Labour movement was to create and harness power for it, and by constantly stating the trades unions' point of view keep the Labour Party's feet on the ground'.

It makes one wonder what is the point of the modern Labour Party, and where exactly its feet are placed.

We should not be fooled by Attlee's apparent modesty. He was well aware of his worth and intelligence. As Christopher Hollis observed,

> 'In a world in which so many people pretend to be more important than they are, the British people has, I think, shown its wisdom and generosity in taking to its heart a man who spends his time pretending to be less important than he his.'[4]

Nick Matthews

References
1 Atlee, Kenneth Harris, Weidenfeld and Nicholson, London, 1982,p10
2 Atlee, Kenneth Harris, Weidenfeld and Nicholson, London, 1982, p33.
3 As It Happened, C.R.Attlee, William Heinemann, 1954, pp33&34.
4 Attlee, Kenneth Harris, Weidenfeld and Nicholson, London, 1982, p553.

Saving Capitalism?

Ha-Joon Chang, *23 Things They Don't Tell You About Capitalism*, Allen Lane, 304 pages, hardback ISBN 9781846143281, £20

The basic assumption of this clever little book is that capitalism has taken a wrong route since the 1980s, in embracing totally the so-called 'neo-liberal' faith in the unregulated global market. Chang, who is a Reader in the Political Economy of Development at Cambridge University, has identified 23 ways in which, so we are frequently told, globalised capitalism works to produce a more effective and better world economy. All of these he demonstrates are manifestly false. The list of what Chang calls the 23 'things', which are false, is an interesting one, and worth recapitulating:

There is no such thing as a free market. Companies should not be run in the interest of the owners. The washing machine has changed the world (for women – MBB) more than the Internet. Assume the worst about people, and you get the worst. Macro-economic stability has not made the world more stable. Free market policies rarely make poor countries rich. Capital is national. We do not live in a post-industrial age. The US does not have the highest living standard in the world. Africa is not destined for under-development. Governments can pick winners. Making rich people richer does not make us all richer. US managers are over-priced. People in poor countries are more entrepreneurial than people in rich countries. We are not smart enough to leave things to the market. More education in itself is not going to make a country richer. What is good for General Motors is not necessarily good for the United States. Despite the fall of Communism, we are not living in planned economies. Equality of opportunity may not be fair. Big government makes people more open to change. Financial markets need to become less, not more, efficient. Good economic policy does not require good economists.

This is an odd mix of denials of what goes for contemporary economic wisdom. The most important is the denial, not only of the morality but also of the effectiveness, of reliance on the free global market, with minimal government interference. Chang has the evidence of the financial and economic crisis, first of the late 1990s and then of 2008-9, to support his view. And it is incredible that anyone should go on believing that, after the latest crisis, the old free market system can be revived. Chang's book should be a useful antidote.

What is missing in the book, however, is a more fundamental criticism of capitalism. Chang assumes that capitalism could be made to work, with less reliance on the market and less financial activity, and more state intervention and regulation. But capitalism resists regulation and generates inequality – between owners of capital and wage slaves – and inequality generates financial activity including increasing speculation. All that there was, which for many years restrained capitalist excesses, was the threat of an alternative in the Soviet Union. When that collapsed in the 1980s, it was just then that capital owners felt free to open up the market, let inequality increase, and financial speculation run riot.

There is now nothing to stop this happening again. Indeed, at the end of 2010 we can already see it happening. There are no wage slaves' movements of revolt that seem likely to create a political atmosphere in which Chang's proposals for income redistribution, state regulation and financial control could be introduced in any of the developed capitalist economies, or in those developing such as China, India and Brazil. All are desperately looking to protect themselves individually from the worst effects of a rotten system. A fundamental challenge to capitalism, such as Marx envisaged, seems even more remote. Perhaps, the threat of climate change to the whole survival of the planet might alter things, but this is an eventuality that Chang does not consider, and there are clear signs that the deniers of planetary disaster believe that somehow they, or the better placed among them, can survive in a world where half the population is dying.

The fact is that there are another two or three things, in addition to Chang's 23, which they do not tell you about capitalism. The first is that the system has no built-in means for changing course. (Marx believed that an organised working class would provide that; it didn't.) And the second is that capitalism's reliance on the competitive instinct in human beings is undervaluing the co-operative instinct which alone might ensure the planet's survival. A third and fundamental omission is any denial of the popular view of capitalism that human beings are made up of a few very clever and imaginative ones and a large number of much less clever and less imaginative, and recognition rather of a very wide range of different kinds of cleverness and imagination which just need the opportunity to express themselves. Such opportunities are simply not created by the workings of capitalism; indeed they are very widely suppressed by poverty, ill heath and lack of education in a majority of the world's population, even including at least a quarter of those in the most developed capitalist economies. A massive attack on these evils might make a big difference. So, we had better concentrate on that.

Michael Barratt Brown

Housing

Sarah Glynn (editor), Where the other half lives: lower income housing in a neoliberal world, Pluto Press, 224 pages, hardback ISBN 978-0745328584, £60, paperback ISBN 9780745328577 £17.99

Neoliberalism hastens a return to unfettered market provision of housing and the uncontrolled physical development of urban space. There are two forms: so-called 'roll-back' and 'roll-out' neoliberalism. The first, the roll-back version, involves reducing the role of the state through active promotion of individual purchase of public housing or mass stock transfer to private or semi-private organisations. The second, the 'roll-out' version, extends market principles into public housing provision in various ways: increasing public rents to market/near-market levels; reducing security of tenure or making it conditional (on having paid work, for example); using the insecurity generated by clearance programmes to contain dissent and protest against 'regeneration' (gentrification) of potentially lucrative parts of cities or towns.

The first part of this collection provides more detail about what the editor, Sarah Glynn, calls 'the neoliberal project', and also a theoretical grounding (in a form of élite theory), which is taken up to varying degrees by the other contributors. This is followed by accounts from England, Scotland, France, Sweden, New Zealand, Australia, the United States and Canada. These countries are all older industrialized ones from North West Europe and the 'Anglophone nations'. They share many 'basic characteristics' and are 'frequently used as models of neo-liberalism', especially in relation to development models being promoted in Eastern Europe and Russia (p5). The case-study authors each give a brief outline of their country's housing policy to provide sufficient context for the more detailed account of how the physical and social fabric of their city, region or country is being transformed by the practical implementation of neoliberal approaches to housing. They also emphasize the resistance to these changes, where this exists. This links into the remaining two chapters of the book, which focus on ways in which neoliberal practices have been or are being challenged.

It is only possible to give the briefest indication here of the detail of the eight case-study chapters which form the core of the book, and its strength. Cumulatively, they show that public assets in the form of social or public housing, land and amenities are immensely valuable not just as commodities (which is the neoliberal view) but also in relation to working class culture, politics, education and health. These collectively-owned assets have been and are under considerable threat in all the countries included in this book.

In the United States, the tiny public sector has been subject to 'roll-back' and 'roll-out' neoliberal policy interventions since the 1980s. The current HOPE VI programme (described in detail) embodies substantial demolition of public housing; linking security of tenure to work in various ways; giving vouchers to tenants for them to use in finding private rented housing when homes are demolished rather than rehousing them in public housing; transferring responsibility for management (including increased powers of eviction) from federal government to public housing authorities (PHAs) which are far from accountable. If this represents the extreme, strong resonances can be seen in all the accounts from other countries.

In England and Scotland, mass stock transfer to the semi-private and private sectors has been pursued by Conservative and New Labour governments since 1980, along with substantial stock loss through the promotion of individual tenant purchase (the 'right to buy'). The detailed case-studies of Leeds and Dundee respectively analyse the implementation of a housing Private Finance Initiative scheme and describe how 'regeneration' is being used as a cover for gentrification of Dundee into the 'City of Discovery'.

From the 1990s, New Zealand also experienced an extreme version of 'roll out' neoliberalism (mass stock transfer, individual sales, market rents) but this country provides evidence that there may be political limitations to 'the neoliberal project'. Since 2000, the approach has 'softened': rental affordability is now a political issue. There is similar evidence from other countries where political administrations have changed political hue (for example, in Ontario, Canada). But, of course, in England, New Labour has been succeeded by a Conservative/Liberal coalition government which is pursuing this path with even more determination.

The changes to the housing systems described in this book are substantial. Opposing and reversing them is a difficult task. For this reason, the contributors have provided substantial detail about opposition to these changes: initiatives, campaigning and information sources. These are very valuable resources for tenants' groups, activists and academics concerned to change what is happening through activism, teaching and writing.

Cathy Davis

Keir Hardie

Bob Holman, *Keir Hardie – Labour's Greatest Hero?*, Lion Hudson plc, 224 pages, paperback ISBN 9780745953540, £10.99

A while ago, I was watching Newsnight Scotland when who should appear but Bob Holman. It was at the time of Iain Duncan Smith's announcement of his 'biggest shake-up' of the welfare system since Beveridge. Bob was somehow persuaded to do some work for Duncan Smith's Centre for Social Justice. Now, there's an Orwellian title for a Tory think-tank. It would probably be close to the mark if I interpreted Bob's response as being horrified at the thought that his participation could in any way be accepted as some sort of support for that old Tory slander that the victims of unemployment should be punished for their condition.

Bob Holman has recently published a very readable biography of Keir Hardie, 'Labour's Greatest Hero?' Hardy was indeed well aware of the capacity of the capitalist political system to incorporate leading working class spokespersons to add credibility and breadth to their appeal to the electorate. In fact, Bob provides an acute analysis of two aspects of Hardie's intellectual make-up which were affected by this dichotomy. These were his Christian beliefs and his socialist commitments. Sadly, it is a truism that many churchgoers profess Christian beliefs but do not behave as Christians, and many members of the Labour Party proclaim their support for socialism, but don't ask them to support it in office.

Hardie's pursuit of both sources of hypocrisy was never diverted by naivety; when it came to firing arrows of derision at the pious factory owner he rarely missed his target. He also was a marksman of pinpoint accuracy when it came to those who took the Lib-Lab shilling, which strangely made them lose their tongues when it came to condemning mine owners who placed profits before miners' safety. Bob Holman provides much well researched material from newspaper articles, some of which appeared in Hardie's own *Labour Leader*.

Hardie never got round to producing an autobiography, although there have been several biographies. Bob's is different in many ways in that he explores the difficulties and deprivations confronting Keir Hardie, and his long suffering wife Lillie, as he pursued his peaceful social revolution without regular resources to do so. Holman also provides an antidote to the lies of the Tory and Liberal press barons about Hardie's supposed wealth and his dourness. Unsurprisingly, Hardie did enjoy a good ceilidh, but in the company of his ain folk.

Hardie left his home in Cumnock to his family, as well as the £96 still due from his parliamentary salary. Doesn't this put the recent corruption of parliament robbing the public through their expenses claims all in some perspective? What would Hardie have said today? He probably wouldn't have been allowed into the Party, and, even if he was, the careerists would not have allowed him anywhere near the leadership.

In 1898, at the Independent Labour Party conference, Keir Hardie expounded the Party's attitude to armed conflict:

'War in the past was inevitable when the sword constituted the only court of appeal. But the old reasons for war have passed away, and, the reasons gone, war should go also. Today they fight to extend markets, and no empire can stand based solely on the sordid considerations of trade and commerce. This is running the empire on the lines of an huckster's shop, and making our statesmen glorified bagmen.'

What would Hardy say of Blair's visit to India to sell arms on behalf of BAE, or four Coalition ministers visiting China on a sales mission to the country that already has everything including our debt?

Hardie had a great interest in international affairs and, for a man of his class, was well travelled, having attended the great socialist international conferences and made the acquaintance of the great socialist leaders of his time. I have a picture in my mind of the delegates at the Second International in Paris, in 1889, turning in their seats to see who it was that had just introduced himself as the delegate on behalf of the Ayrshire Miners. It is sad to think that we now have Labour Members of the European Parliament, fully funded, who, unlike Hardie, can be in Brussels in an hour. In a century's time, will they have a Bob Holman reaching for his pen and finding a rich and inspiring story like that of the illegitimate Scottish miner who founded a political movement against all the odds? What, indeed, would Hardie say?

Henry McCubbin

Credit Crunch

John Bellamy Foster and Fred Magdoff, *The Great Financial Crisis: Causes and Consequences*, Monthly Review Press 2009, 160 pages, paperback ISBN 9781583671849, £10.95

At one level this book could be seen as an important extension of the ideas of Paul A. Baran and Paul M. Sweezy as published in their 1966 classic work, *Monopoly Capital*. The book attempts to bring up to date Baran and Sweezy's thinking in the light of the neo-liberal counter-revolution and the metamorphosis of capitalism itself. The focus of the book is still, however, the present crisis, universally known as the 'Credit Crunch'. In fact, as a demonstration of the perspicacity of the authors, the first four chapters are taken from previous issues of *Monthly Review* magazine over the period May 2006 to April 2007, with only the two final chapters written specifically for the book. Unlike our exalted leaders, the authors clearly saw that the debt bubble was about to burst.

In order to place the book in the correct context, therefore, it is necessary to touch briefly upon the basic ideas of Baran and Sweezy. Their fundamental appraisal of capitalism after the depression of the 1930s and the conclusion of the Second World War was that competitive market capitalism had been transformed into 'monopoly capitalism': a capitalism determined by giant corporations, mainly US, who no longer competed through cut-throat price competition but orchestrated an oligopolistic competitive market through internal cost-cutting, marketing, and product innovation, together with increased productivity, often utilising improved production methods. This process led to the accumulation of large surpluses which, given capitalism's insatiable proclivities, restlessly aspired to multiply through further profitable investment. By the late 1960s, such investment was beginning to look decidedly thin. This form of managed capitalism, which manipulated sector pricing and other factors, had resulted in productive overcapacity, and hence a difficult environment for profitable investment. This led to a generalised stagnation of the economy with real wages insufficient to take up the slack. Therefore, in spite of temporary booms followed by bust, the normal state of capitalism is one of stagnation through under-consumption.

The only solution for this stagnation malaise was the extension of credit on a massive scale, and to areas where it was previously largely absent at an organised corporate level – to the working and lower middle classes. Credit cards and store cards were handed out like confetti whilst, in the financial centres, innovative and arcane techniques for making money out of money were devised: the hedge fund, derivatives, futures, leveraged buyouts, etc. For the authors, this new twist to the economic situation, as described above, means that debt is now such an integral part of the system that they consider 'monopoly capitalism' has become 'monopoly finance capital'. Necessarily, they now investigate the growth of personal and corporate debt in the context of the US economy in some detail, plus the mechanisms and consequences of 'financialisation'.

Naturally enough, the first chapter discusses the problem of household debt and the sub-prime mortgage débâcle in the context of the ever-increasing structural wage inequality found in the US workforce. Since the late 1970s, equipped with their neo-liberal 'insights', Thatcher and Reagan had imposed what David Harvey has called a regime of 'wage repression' so that, by the start of the credit binge, real wages had fallen, and they have remained repressed to the present day. Examining the conundrum of falling real wages and yet no reciprocal fall in consumer spending, the authors insist that the shortfall could only be made up through borrowing. Of course, this extension of mortgage credit was predicated on ever-rising prices in the housing market, but also the 'securitisation' of this debt through a piece of financial sleight of hand, using a novel instrument called the collateralised debt obligation (CDO). The latter wizardry was only one in a whole series of innovative financial free market devices calculated to allow increased indebtedness whilst deferring the consequences.

The Great Financial Crisis provides real insights into the explosion of speculation and debt in the US economy, which began its precipitous rise at the beginning of the 1980s. What the authors mean by financialisation is a switch from the making of profits mainly by producing goods to, primarily, profits being made out of finance itself, so that by 2005 financial profits as a percentage of total US domestic profits constituted 40%. The book touches on the connection between the US defence industry, the new strident imperialism and an America which wishes to secure economic hegemony over other trade blocs and secure raw material supply, (in particular oil), and how this fits into the overall financialisation picture.

In general, The Great Financial Crisis does suffer from a degree of US parochialism in the sense that the present crisis cannot be understood completely from a US only perspective. There is, for instance, no discussion of the rivalry between advanced industrialised nations. Another possible weakness is that the under-consumption thesis regarding capitalism has been criticised for mixing up cause and effect. Other Marxists have come up with alternative theories for the continuing malaise of capitalism. Robert Brenner has identified overproduction and overcapacity of manufacturing worldwide, leading to low investment and falling profits. What we can all hopefully agree on is that we are facing, as the book would describe it, a capitalism that, whilst still having its fundamental drives intact, has metamorphosed yet again from monopoly capital to monopoly finance capital. Manufacturing, certainly in the United States and Britain at least, has lost its primacy, and the paramount role in profit-making is now finance in its many forms. This is particularly noticeable in the case of Britain where the willingness to please the 'City' seems to be mandatory for the media and politicians, at the expense of investment in manufacturing industry.

Without a doubt, the financial élite, after a brief dalliance with Keynesianism, seems determined to return to the old habits. The Great Financial Crisis provides the clarity to expose that élite's insatiable appetites and resist its drive to make us all pay for its profligacy. It is one of many stimulating accounts on the present crisis from the Marxist and other points of view. It is definitely one of the clearest expositions of the continuing credit crisis, and deserves to be read for the comprehensiveness of its approach as well as the cogency of its argument.

John Daniels

Armenia

Jo Laycock, *Imagining Armenia: Orientalism, Ambiguity and Intervention*, Manchester University Press, 258 pages, hardback ISBN 9780719078170, £60

It is a challenging task to choose a pictorial or graphic front page/jacket image for a book with a title such as the above. Yet Lois Raemaekers' *Detail from Armenia* of 1917 somehow sets the tone for the contents and conclusions of this book. It is the image of a corpulent mother figure, with scarf covered head, in a quasi Rodin-esque thinking pause, lost in the dilemma of her whereabouts and 'what to do next', with her youngster beside her facing the onlooker with bewildered eyes piercing the unknown. Raemaekers' image, which appeared then as *The Lord Mayor of London Appeals for Help* poster, is also reproduced in the book. As if delineating this same image, Joanne Laycock, now a Post-doctoral Fellow in Armenian Studies at the University of Michigan concludes her impressive study, saying:

> Despite the coming of independence in 1991 the ambiguous image of Armenia is still embedded in complex power relations as Armenia continues to negotiate a place in the post-Soviet world. (p.228)

Perusing the *Introduction*, I felt Laycock was very much engulfed in the condescending aura of some of the Armenian American historians emulating bygone *Orientalists*, those targeted by E. Said's criticism. She has quoted (p.5) the following characteristic remark of R.G. Suny:

> Often directed toward an 'ethnic' rather than a broader international or scholarly audience, Armenian historical writing has been narrowly concerned with fostering a positive view of an endangered nationality ... Criticsm has been avoided as if it might aid present enemies and certain kinds of inquiry have been shunned as betrayels of the national cause. (*Constructing Primordialism*, p. 2)

No surprise, then, the absence from this study of Armenian history written in the Armenian language the exception being the Russian edition of A. J. Kirakossian's *Great Britain and the Armenian Question:1890s*, published in Yerevan in 1990, and the same Kirakossian as editor to *The Armenian Massacres, 1894-1896*, published in Detroit in 2004. Also, Laycock's last Chapter, *Post-war Armenia*, has three quotes from British Aid workers, found in the Armenian National Archives which leads the Primary Souces, abbreviated in the *Notes* as NAA.

My initial impression, though, did somehow yield its relevance to the impact I gathered from the multi-layered construction of her thesis. She has essentially examined the portrayal in Britain of Armenia and the Armenians during the 19th and 20th centuries. Hence, she could have probably felt in tune with some aspects of Levon A. Bayramian's pioneering book in Armenian, published in Yerevan in 1982, entitled *Western Armenia in The Plans of English Imperialism.* Yet Bayramian's book is an absentee from Laycock's study.

Before Said's *Orientalism* became a houshold name in Academia, a couple of Armenian writers did indulge in classifying aspects of what 'others' – non Armenians – have presented Armenia and the Armenians, the latter being in their own turn the 'other' to the non Armenians, as, for example, *Armenia Observed*, ed. by Ara Baliozian (1979), and *As Others See Us*, by Leo Hamalian (1980), both in English. Christopher Waker's *Visions of Ararat* (1997), a collection of exclusively British writing on Armenia, was a welcome addition to the genre. The latter book has deserved a mention as 'a notable exception' by Laycock in her *Introduction* (p.4).

While recording nineteenth century impressions of Armenian architecture, including the admiration of Layard (*Discoveries*, 1850, p.33) and Lynch (*Armenia*, 1902, p.371), Jo Laycock has felt the importance of mentioning, in her corresponding *Notes* (p.92), the work of Josef Strsygovski, the noted Viennese professor. But, alas, the matter is discussed without the crucial Armenian primary source.

The renowned architect and scholar of antiquities, Toros Toramanian (1864-1934), was a pioneer of architectural studies in Armenia during the late 19th century and early 1900s. It is a well known fact that Toramanian met Strsygovski twice, in Vienna and in Armenia, handing over most of his architectural research sketches and copious manuscripts of his studies to Strsygovsky, long before the appearance of the latter's monumental work, *Die Baukunst Der Armenier und Europe*, of 1918. Strsygovsky failed to indicate that major source of his research, and his work is labelled by Christina Moranci as:

> highly political and offensive work which linked Indo-European thought to Architecture. (*Medieval Armenian Architecture*, p. 1, quoted by Jo Laycock, p. 92).

The necessity of such criticism was long overdue since the entrenchment of William Jones' pronouncement of 1786 that European and Indian languages such as Greek, Latin and Sanskrit must have sprung from a common proto-language, hence the name *Indo-European*. As language and architecture were thought to exemplify both national and cultural identities, the concept of a proto-language became a major attraction for Orientalist discourse, including Strsygovsky's.

Yet, Toramanian, whose remaining research manuscripts and sketches were postumously published – entitled *Armenian Architecture,* by the Armenian SSR Academy, Yerevan, in two munumental volumes, 1942 (v.1), 1948, (v.2) – specifically mentions the following in his own introductory notes:

> It is obvious that nothing decisive yet exists pertaining the proto-language of today's many existing languages, but for which hypothetical assumptions more than certainties abound. (v 2, p.3):

Such crucial differences of opinion between primary sources indicate the importance of not neglecting Armenian original sources, such as Toramanian and many others, especially when dealing with, and even *imagining* about, a country, its people and its culture. That might have perhaps somehow lessened the projected *ambiguity* of the tale, even when narrated skillfully through the notes of 'others', distinguished as they were.

Significantly, Laycock's *Imagining Armenia* is an imaginative study of the permutations of the concept of the 'other' in relation to Britain and Armenia during a turbulent historical period, culminating in the First World War and the genocide of the Armenians. She uses, perhaps unwittingly, but surely with much profit, what Edward Said, the renowned author of *Orientalism* (1978), had suggested in his *Culture and Imperialism* (1994) to read history and culture 'contrapuntally'. Laycock's contrapuntal analysis of her theses is enlightening, notwithstanding occasional repetitions of the same in various chapters as if paying her debt to counterpoint's initial style of 'imitation'.

Imagining Armenia consists of an introduction, five chapters and a conclusion. With all the scholarly sophistication, judiciously manipulated to write her book, the author has not failed to tell us a fascinating story about a land, a country and its people as percieved and portrayed, often with ambiguity, by the British, whether writers, travellers, historians, philanthropers and government officials, not forgetting the effect of the contradictory colonial politics of the British empire on the destiny of the land called Armenia and the future of its people, the Armenians.

Khatchatur I. Pilikian

Keep Talking

Mark Perry, *How to Lose the War on Terror*, Hurst Publishers 2010, 270 pages, hardback ISBN 9781850659624, £37.45, paperback ISBN 9781850659631, £12.99

This is a book which gets more and more interesting as the pages turn. It started life as a series of articles in the *Asian Times* in 2005. Then it developed into a book project when the author became involved, in 2005 and 2006, in attempts to dialogue with the Sunni resistance in northern Iraq. It became a full-blown book after further involvement with Hamas and Hezbollah leaders in Palestine and Lebanon.

The message which runs through it all is clear: 'Jaw Jaw is better than War War'. Perhaps, granted the hints now emerging from Afghanistan of talks with the Taliban, we are beginning, at last, to learn that lesson there. We ought to have learnt it decades ago during the Northern Ireland civil war.

The book starts with a very good quotation from that remarkable historian Barbara Tuchman:

'To halt the momentum of an accepted idea, to re-examine assumptions, is a disturbing process and requires more courage than Governments can usually summon'.

The entrenched idea in this case is that military power can defeat armed resistance which has some level of popular support. It can't. Sooner or later there have to be talks with 'the enemy'. There are always differing political aims, which have to be faced. Slapping labels on insurgents and calling them terrorists only manufactures yet more real terrorists.

The author's experience in Northern Iraq several years after the 2003 invasion is fascinating. It was, in fact, the United States military and the Civil Affairs group who responded to an invitation from some influential Iraqi exiles in Amman. Their up-front aim was to help to rebuild the Iraqi economy, but discussions went much further than that. So far, in fact, that hostile but significant people such as Paul Wolfowitz slammed down the shutters with a vengeance and humiliated the officials involved. His understanding of the situation, and I am sure others shared his ideas, was simple: 'Don't you know that these people are all Nazis'?

The official United States line was that there could be no talks with those they defined as terrorists. That is not even true according to their own past practice. The PLO and ANC and the opposition in Iraq were all called terrorists in their time, but US discussions went on with them nevertheless.

The chapters on Hamas, Hezbollah and Israel all tell the same story. There is an interesting quotation from a senior Hamas leader about the explicit clause in their Charter calling for the destruction of Israel, which is hardly compatible, anyway, with the Hamas offer of a ten-year truce. Says he: 'The Charter is not the Koran - it can be amended'.

There might have been a very different story to tell about the Middle East if the United States had not mounted such heavy opposition to the democratic result of the 2006 Palestinian elections. All CIA stops, at the orders of President Bush, were pulled out to make a Fatah/Hamas partnership impossible. Hamas leaders wanted to talk but their terrorist label made that impossible. Condoleezza Rice's staff were clear. The Secretary of State 'doesn't talk to terrorists'.

Probably all readers of this book will begin to wonder if we are not following much the same path as that of the United States. Islamaphobia is now spreading in Britain. Many Muslims see themselves as a people under threat. Expulsions and imprisonment, or the indefinite house prison of control orders, without knowledge of accuser or accusations, are now normal. Yet this is in the land of *Habeas Corpus*. If Bin Laden is still alive he must be delighted. There is no better way to provide him with more local recruits. Those responsible, at Government level, for our security would do well to read Mark Perry's interesting book.

Bruce Kent

A Dodo?

Philip Atkins and Michael Johnson *A Dodo at Oxford: The Unreliable Account of a Student and his pet Dodo*, Oxgarth Press, 160 pages, hardback ISBN 978 0 9534438 2 6, £12.99

The apparent mystery surrounding the origins and authenticity of this book's contents made it intriguing from the first page. Supposedly an investigation of a diary, written in 1695 by an Oxfordshire man about his pet Dodo then rediscovered in a charity shop in 2008, it is initially quite plausible with its aesthetically realistic photographs of diary pages and early modern typography. The mystery disappears relatively quickly upon reading however, raising the question of the book's purpose. Whilst the diary itself is almost certainly nothing more than an entertaining ruse, the accompanying commentary contains much historical fact and amusing observation. Is this merely a bizarre self-indulgence or perhaps an intellectual in-joke? One has to wonder quite how small the niche market will be for the punchline. Whatever the intention of the authors the book remains an entertaining, if slightly bemusing, journey through the life of a man and his dodo in early modern Oxfordshire, interspersed with the dissection of random contemporary artefacts 'discovered' in the diary. At the end of the book, despite the smiles raised along the way, one question remains – why?

Sarah O'Malley

Afghanistan

Bob Woodward, *Obama's Wars – The Inside Story*, Simon & Schuster 2010, 464 pages, ISBN 9780857200440, £20

Even though this book is really only about one war – Afghanistan – it is a very revealing story. More than that, it is also an astonishing one for reasons that the author would not have had in mind. The dysfunctional relationship between the White House and the Pentagon, which this book reveals, is quite scary. These are the same people who make nuclear weapon decisions.

The book is a blow-by-blow, meeting-by-meeting account of the way in which, during 2009, a policy was agreed which resulted in Obama's statement about Afghanistan of November 2009. He announced then, after all these discussions, that there would be a troop increase (not as large as the Pentagon wanted) and, most significantly, the start of a military withdrawal in July 2011.

There are several surprises. Since Afghanistan is meant to be a UN/NATO operation, no one seems to have thought of consulting their so-called partners in the run-up to this decision. Ban Ki- Moon does not even appear in the index. British forces get the briefest mention. Even so, they get more than is given to those of the other countries with troops deployed.

Solutions to problems are overwhelmingly framed in military terms. 'The man who is equipped only with a hammer sees every problem as a nail' rings true on every page. Obama, with Vietnam in mind, is clearly desperate to get out of the Afghanistan swamp. He is, however, squeezed at every point by the military. His Vice-President, Joe Biden, has, perhaps, the most original ideas, but he gets marginalized.

There is no evidence that any one realises that the United States is not thought, by the rest of the world, to be God's gift to world order. No one asks why terrorists take to terrorism or if insurgents have some reason for insurging – if I may invent a word. At one point, even an intelligent man like the President himself says 'We don't seek world domination or occupation'. The 1,000 US bases and military facilities strung around the world tell a different story to most of us.

US connivance in the occupation of Palestine or the slaughter in Iraq, as reasons for Muslim hostility, gets no mention. Palestine itself is not even in the index. It is indeed revealing that Pakistan, with its eyes on India, has played such an ambivalent role in the whole conflict.

In a rather *Readers' Digest* style the author describes in detail all the various lengthy top level meetings that went on before the November announcement. I had to wonder how Obama sleeps at night, and when he has time to think about the other pressing problems on his mind.

Thankfully, the book starts with a helpful list of all the participants, military, diplomatic and White House. The reader is left with no idea where the lines of authority actually run. Loyalty to the President, much trumpeted, is actually in short supply. Time and again the military come back to challenge his views with amendments, alternative suggestions and even media contradictions. This habit is not just a military weakness. Robert Gates, Secretary of Defence, tells a dinner gathering in Washington, at which President Karzai is present, 'we are not leaving Afghanistan prematurely ... in fact we are not leaving at all'. This was exactly the opposite of the Obama position, which all had agreed to support. General Petraeus, the new commander in Afghanistan, says more privately, 'this is the kind of fight we're in for the rest of our lives and probably our kids' lives'.

This is a very important book which ought to be studied carefully. It is not the details of the discussions that matter or the pecking order of in-fights amongst the military, of which there are plenty. What it reveals is how the most powerful country in the world in military terms actually makes up its mind on critical international issues. The United Nations is a distant sideshow, as are the rest of us. NATO, an arm of US policy, is simply a means of disguising the reality.

The book has, too, a sad taste of tragedy. A decent man, suddenly given great world power, who knows where he wants to go, is impeded, but not yet brought to a halt, by forces, military and political, which are more powerful than he is.

Bruce Kent

HAIKU

Vale, Louis Macneice

who rather drily
asked, 'Am I supposed to by
dying?' (his last words)

Beddoes To Beckett

Thought from *Death's Jest-Book*:
'What is the lobster's tune when
he is boiling?' – Eh?

Resolute
i.m. Ken Coates

One more good man gone!
Haiku he liked – hence, alas,
this briefest tribute.

*Alexis Lykiard's fine new collection, **Haiku at Seventy**, is published by Anarchio Press, price £8 (www.alexislykiard.com).*